# New Bells for New Steeples

## Communication Strategies
## for Building Parish Community

### Jay Cormier

Sheed & Ward

Sheed & Ward™ is a service of National Catholic Reporter Publishing
Company, Inc.

Library of Congress Card Number: 90-62651

ISBN: 1-55612-369-8

Published by:     Sheed & Ward
                  115 E. Armour Blvd. P.O. Box 419492
                  Kansas City, MO 64141-6492

To order, call: (800) 333-7373

*For Martin, Ben, Gabriel and Brad,*
*and for Elizabeth and Joseph*

# Contents

# Preface

Only a part of a project like this is the result of research and a study of the literature in the field.

A great deal of the practical material and insights contained in these pages have been collected, tried and sometimes tried again (and again) in actual church settings. The author, therefore, prefaces this book with a word of gratitude for the opportunity to serve in the communications offices of the Diocese of Manchester (New Hampshire), the Archdiocese of Washington, D.C., and Merrimack College (North Andover, Mass.). I am grateful that I had the chance to work with many wonderful people who allowed me to both succeed and fail, learning from both experiences.

I would also like to thank Rev. Thomas Bresnahan and the parishioners of my own parish community of St. Mark the Evangelist in Londonderry, N.H. Father Bresnahan's own insights as a pastor, his friendship and his affording me the opportunity to work with the parish leadership were starting points for much of what follows.

During the actual writing and editing of this volume, I was fortunate to have the support and encouragement of my present employer, the Episcopal Diocese of Massachusetts. I am deeply grateful to Bishop David Johnson and my friends and co-workers at "138 Tremont" for their support, help, and for more than one good idea and insight that appear in these pages.

Many, many good friends contributed everything from a much sought-after piece of documentation to an encouraging word when the relationship between this project and its creator were particularly strained. Although their names are far too many to include here, without their contributions this project would never have been completed.

I am especially grateful to Dr. Meredith Handspicker of Andover Newton Theological School for his guidance, counsel and his enthusiastic "shepherding" of this project. My thanks, too, to Dr.

Eddie S. O'Neal of Andover Newton and Dr. Ann Morgan of Boston College who served as members of the committee.

I would also like to acknowledge the invaluable contribution made by a group of pastors and communications professionals who reviewed and evaluated this project. I am most grateful to Rev. Denis Audet, Curtis Barnes, Rev. Robert Biron, Susan Husted, Rev. W. Ronald Jameson, the Rev. Christopher Moore, Rev. Philip Murnion, Jean Nero and Rev. Miles O'Brien Riley, whose challenging insights and suggestions made the pages you have in your hand now far better than they were in earlier drafts.

No undertaking like this ever sees the light of day without the support, care and more than a little patience from the writer's family. This writer has been especially blessed in this regard. These few words do not begin to express the depth of my love and gratitude to my wife and best friend, Ann.

# Introduction

For centuries, the bells tolling from church steeples called the faithful to prayer and worship, proclaimed the beginning and the end of the work day and announced news of joy and sorrow to the community.

The technology of communications has advanced light-years beyond the tolling bell. Today's parishioners are part of the most media-aware and media "assaulted" generation of all time. Growing up with television, satellites and computers, they have never known a time when they could not be instantaneously "plugged in" to events anywhere in the world. This media awareness affects both the quality and quantity of the messages an audience receives (one striking example: how television has conditioned a generation to receiving news and information in short, visually exciting pieces).

Catholic parishes, in particular, have had some difficulty in adapting their communications programs to this reality. Today's Catholic population is more mobile than previous generations. Catholicism is no longer exclusively the "immigrants' church," made up of homogeneous, neighborhood parishes. Today's Catholics are part of the mainstream of American society, reflecting a pluralism of belief and philosophy and a diversity of culture, ethnicity and race. These changes within the Catholic community necessitate new and more sophisticated approaches in communicating both within the Church itself and with society at-large.

In other words, new "bells" are needed for today's parish "steeples." This book is designed to help pastors and ministers "connect" with their parish communities through these new technologies and research in communications.

This volume has been written and edited to serve as a communications "handbook" to give pastors

- an understanding of the communication process: how messages are "decoded" by an audience and the factors that can expedite or distort a message's goal;

- a vision of today's parish community as a "community of communities," an assembly of distinct groups, each having different expectations and needs from the Church, and the most effective ways to communicate with each group; and

- practical strategies for building parish community through effective communications techniques.

After each of the six chapters, a "workshop" section is included. These workshops are designed to challenge pastors to apply the strategies discussed to their own parish situations, as well as to introduce and sharpen specific communications skills.

By incorporating the communications strategies discussed here into their pastoral planning, pastors should be able to "look" at their parish communities in new ways, enabling them to recognize new and unrealized opportunities available to them to bring parishioners together. A primary goal of this book is to raise awareness among church leadership of the importance of well-planned, sophisticated communications strategies in fulfilling the Church's mission to proclaim the Gospel and build the body of Christ.

One additional note: While written from the author's Roman Catholic perspective and experience, this book may also be of use to non-Catholic parishes, to those responsible for the "church at-large" (bishops, denominational executives) and to specialized church agencies and communities.

Also, the use of such words and phrases as "pastor," "parish communicator" and "minister" in the text are interchangeable and should be read to include any leader or minister serving a church community, agency or organization.

# Chapter 1

# The Communications Process:
# The Model

In an episode of the comic strip "The Wizard of Id," the King visits the site of Id's new space project. "How's the Royal Space Project progressing?" the diminutive monarch inquires.

The head technician explains, "We've run into a problem. There's been a major malfunction of the primary propulsion system in the first stage vehicle."

"What does that mean?" the mystified King asks.

A worker in the back pipes up, "It means the rubber band broke."

Simply put, human communication is the process of creating meaning between two people.[1] The word "communication" is derived from the Latin "communicare"—"to make common." The effectiveness of communication, then, is measured in one's ability to obtain a common understanding of an idea. Communication takes place when the stimulus, as it was intended by the sender, corresponds with the stimulus perceived and responded to by the intended audience.[2]

Most leaders say they recognize the importance of communication in making their organizations work, but surprisingly few understand how the communication process itself *works*. At its many levels of structure and organization, the Church has had a particularly difficult time integrating communications into its mission and ministries. For the most part, the Church has mastered one-direction message-sending, communicating from "shepherd" (the hierarchy and clergy) *down* to "sheep" (the laity).

But the mere act of issuing a volume of words directed "at" a given group of people is no longer a guarantee that the message will have any meaningful effect at all. In this high-tech age of mass communications, we are bombarded with messages from many different sources, all competing for our attention. We have become more selective about which messages we will absorb—and which we will tune-out altogether. Organizational message-senders have learned not to take communication for granted. They now look for indicators of what impact their messages have had—in other words, all effective communication today flows, not in one direction, but in *two* (or more) directions.

What follows is a "picture" of the communication process. Every act of message-sending—whether a McDonald's television spot, a novel on this week's *The New York Times Best Sellers List*, a letter from a friend, or your parish bulletin—contains all the elements of this model. The effectiveness of the transmission and reception of that message depends on how well the sender understands the dynamics of this model. The first step, then, in becoming an effec-

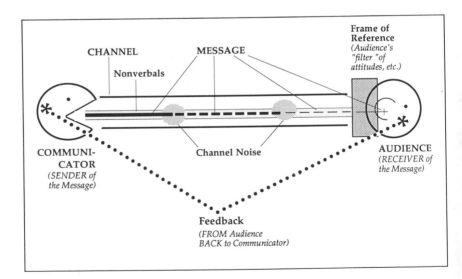

**Fig. 1.** The Communications Process

tive parish communicator is to understand the basic elements of the communications process.

## The Mission: To Affect Behavior

Every act of communicating includes a *communicator* (or transmitter) sending a *message* to an *audience* (or receiver). The communicator originates the message. In order to have any chance at success, the communicator must have a clear idea of the goal of his/her message—and that goal is *behavioral*. The ultimate goal is to present the message so that it has the desired impact on the audience's behavior.[3] The goal may be to get the intended audience to do something specific, such as buying a product or voting for a particular candidate or contributing to a cause; or the goal may be an immediate reaction (evoking their laughter at your story) or to secure their understanding of an event or process (making an audience of high school sophomores understand a multi-step theorem in geometry).

The goal in any communication is to send a message that will have the desired impact on the audience's behavior; in other words, as a result of this message, the audience will act or think as the communicator wants them to.

The importance of clearly defining the message's goal cannot be overstated. Messages often fail to connect with their intended audience because a definite, single objective for the message has not been clearly determined. The result is often a message that is muddled and mixed, with the audience having no clear idea of what is expected of them. In terms of an organization like the Church, communication requires an objective that has been stated and agreed to by all initiators of the process: the sender must understand what the goal is, what message is to be received by what audience, and the desired behavioral response from that audience.[4]

*Before* a message is created, the communicator must focus on

- the effect desired and response sought from the audience;
- the characteristics of the medium (channel) to be used;

- the dynamics between the audience and the medium through which they will receive the message, including the environment, the time they are likely to view or hear the message, and the activity going on as the message is sent;

- the previous experiences of individual members of the audience that can be evoked to generate the response desired.[5]

These concepts will be discussed in greater detail in the pages that follow.

Communications, of course, is at the heart of the Church's ministry and mission. Effective leadership requires the ability to articulate a vision and share that vision with others. That vision and its sharing is at the heart of the message to be communicated. To do that, a church community has to have a clear idea of its aims, its reasons for existing and the different segments of people it is called to serve.

## Coding and Decoding Messages

Once the goal has been determined, the communicator designs the message in a *code* or language that the intended audience will understand or *decode*, resulting in their responding as the communicator hopes.

The message travels through some kind of a *medium* or *channel*. The medium or channel may be spatial (a classroom, a sanctuary), technology-based (a telephone wire, a public address system, a videotape, a printed newspaper or book) or rhetorical (a professor's voice, a letter or epistle).

The challenge to the contemporary Church is to learn *new* codes in which to communicate. Since Vatican II especially, the Church has come to see itself as a "world-church" living in a secularized and pluralistic world, engaging in missionary activity and present in new and diverse cultural fields.[6] In adapting to these new venues the Church must learn new codes in which to speak to different cultures.

Among the codes the Church must learn are those "codes" or languages that are unique to various media. The Church, for example, must learn to "speak" effectively on television, understanding both the possibilities and limits of electronic communications. Just as important to realize is how mass media have affected all the other forms of communications the Church may utilize: the impact of television viewing on the average person's attention span is of critical importance to the homilist; the role of media images in shaping a child's values has obvious implications for the religious educator.

Good communicators also understand how, when and why message channels work as they do. The effective message-sender is aware of what particular channels work best with particular audiences at particular times. Any parish minister paying attention knows, for example, that the time immediately after the final blessing at weekend liturgies is perhaps the worst time to make any kind of appeal.

Not only do the message's actual words or verbals communicate to an audience, but the communicator's *nonverbals* enhance or detract from the message's effectiveness, as well. A homilist's body language and the tone (formal, informal, sarcastic, supportive, patronizing, etc.) of the words he/she uses, the color and paper texture of a brochure, the overall quality of a video production, the stature and authority of the individual sending the message in the estimation of the intended audience are all nonverbal factors affecting an audience's receptivity to a message.

Church communicators must also understand an important reality of this age: *A vision of faith cannot be shared by edict or by the exercise of power or coercion.* It is more an act of persuasion, of creating an enthusiastic and dedicated commitment to a vision because it is right for the times, right for the organization and right for the people affected by the organization. In any communication, some distortion takes place, but the effective communicator who is a *leader* is able to find the right image, the right metaphor, the right code that clarifies the idea and minimizes distortion resulting in the receiver assimilating the message.[7]

## Audience-centered Communications

Every effective communication is *audience-centered*. This concept has been very difficult for many institutions—especially the Church—to grasp. Organizations like the Church that have failed to understand the changing world of their constituencies soon find communications a difficult and frustrating undertaking. The message the Church seeks to communicate, however divinely-inspired and worthy of attention, is meaningless if the message is not received as intended. The communication process, then, begins by understanding the intended audience and what dimensions of their lives will be most affected by the message's goal.

On the practical level, being audience-centered means knowing what "buttons to push" that will make the audience respond to the message; but on a much deeper level, the audience-centered communicator comes to understand and respect the needs and expectations of the audience, realizing their pains, sorrows, joys and hopes, as well as the audience's unique life experiences that have, in all probability, already led to the forming of an attitude or disposition toward the issue in question. A Church leadership that sees itself as "ruling by divine right" will not communicate effectively with many American Catholics; a local leadership that assumes that all parishioners understand the importance of a new policy or project equally may be heading for communications disaster, as well.

Quite simply, effective communications starts where the intended audience is "at," not at the organization's level of understanding and appreciation, nor at the level where the organization believes the audience should be. In the eyes of the intended audience, the communicator must be perceived as possessing knowledge and information that the audience recognizes as valuable and important—the communicator must possess the credibility that translates into obtaining the audience's trust that the communicator understands and appreciates their interests.

Related to the concept of audience centeredness is *audience definition*. Not all messages are intended for an organization's entire potential audience. An effective communication defines the intended or target audience as specifically as possible, and seeks out the channels proven most effective in reaching them. The most effective channel, of course, is the informal, one-to-one meeting in which both the communicator and receiver inform and listen.[8] The more direct and personal the approach, the more likely the communicator will obtain the response sought from the audience.

## Challenges to Message Reception: 'Noise' and Frames of Reference

Two factors at work within the communication process will have considerable effect on an audience's decoding of a message.

The first is *channel noise.* "Noise" is any unwanted sound, anything which garbles or distorts a message.[9] A crackling sound system may garble a homilist's words making it difficult for the congregation to hear exactly what is being said. A poor, blotchy printing job is a form of "noise" in the channel of offset printing, making the parish bulletin difficult to read.

Some forms of channel noise have less to do with the transmission of the message than with its reception: audiences may not be disposed to receiving a message because the church is too hot, the chairs are very uncomfortable, or the solicitation letter for the parish building fund came on the same day as the mortgage, the electric bill, the water bill, the tax bill, the American Express bill, and so on.

A second factor affecting the reception of a message is the audience's *frame of reference.* Every message an audience receives is "filtered" through the "screen" of that audience's knowledge, experience, beliefs, prejudices, biases and values. Keep in mind that an audience is composed of both *individuals,* each with unique and sometimes unpredictable tastes, needs and wants, and *groups,* who share social and cultural identities or hold common beliefs and attitudes; in other words, an audience member's frame of reference is made up of his/her own beliefs and attitudes, as well as beliefs and attitudes he/she shares with other members of the audience.

Consequently, the same code word can be immediately embraced by one audience and totally rejected by another audience because of their different frames of reference. Consider, for example, the concept of Mary, the Mother of God. The code-word "Mary" will, in all probability "filter" through the frame of reference of an older, more traditional segment of the Church as a positive concept. They "decode" Mary as an element of a spirituality they know and trust. But that same code word "Mary" may have a negative or neutral impact on a younger, more liberal audience who views Marian devotionals through their frame of reference as a symbol of an archaic spirituality that has no little or no meaning to them.

As it is being received by its intended audience, a message runs through an obstacle course of *beliefs, attitudes* and *perceptions*. The message's success in negotiating through that course determines whether the message is received correctly or incorrectly, whether the message is accepted or rejected.

*Beliefs* are ideas about what is true or false in the world: some beliefs are based on verifiable truths (facts); others are based on personal belief with less certitude and supported with less compelling evidence (opinions); and still other beliefs are so fixed that they become stereotypes. Some beliefs are fixed and anchored by one's training and childhood experience. The more fixed an audience's beliefs, the more difficult they are to change; the more variable, the more easily they are to alter.[8]

*Attitudes* are tendencies to respond positively or negatively to people, objects or ideas. Attitudes express our preferences, predispositions, reactions and basic judgments.[9] Especially relevant in communications are the audience's attitudes toward the communicator, the subject of the message and the goal of the message.

For those who hold them, attitudes serve four functions:

1. *an ego-defensive function:* some attitudes are held because they help people protect themselves from unflattering truths about themselves or about others who are important to them (by despising homosexuals, for example, some men are able to embrace their own feeling of masculinity and self-worth);

2. *a value-expressive function:* some attitudes express values important to the individual (a person may use only products made from recycled materials because their use demonstrates his/her concern about the environment);

3. *a knowledge function:* some attitudes allow people to better understand events and the people around them; (a voter's dislike for

Richard Nixon helps that person understand the ex-President's participation in the Watergate scandal because, "after all, dislikable people do dislikable things"); and

4. *a utilitarian function*: attitudes help people gain rewards and avoid punishment (an employee adopts the attitude of his/her boss in order to advance in the company).[10]

*Perceptions* are the meaning assigned to a message's verbal and nonverbal elements. It is the process of making sense of an incoming message. *Remember that it is the receiver of the message who ultimately determines its meaning.* The editor of the local newspaer decides whether the news release sent from the local parish is actually news or not. The stockholder decides whether the information contained in the annual report bodes good or ill for the company. The announcement of cutbacks in government programs will be seen as a step forward or a step backward depending on the needs, experiences and attitudes of those who hear the announcement.[11]

The critical task in communications, then, is to design a message that resonates with information already stored within an individual and thereby induces the desired learning or behavioral effect. Such resonance takes place when stimuli (the various elements, verbal and nonverbal, of a message) evoke *meaning* in a listener or viewer. That which the message-sender puts into communication has no meaning in itself; the meaning of communication is what a listener or viewer *takes out* of his/her experience with the communicator's stimuli. The audience's life experiences, as well as expectations of the stimuli they are receiving, interact with the communicator's output in determining the meaning of the communication.[12]

Knowing and understanding an intended audience's system of beliefs, attitudes and perceptions is vitally important if the message is to be received and understood as the sender intends.

## What the Audience Communicates to the Communicator

All communications today is a dialogue.[13] Not only does the sender communicate with the receiver, but the receiver communicates *back* to the sender.  Most people are familiar with the concept of *feedback* as a formal, structured measurement of an audience's reaction to a message (such as surveys, sales figures, television and radio ratings); but feedback is quite often informal and unstructured—and no less important.  The communicant fumbling with the bulletin during the homily, poor attendance at a church function, lukewarm participation in prayer and liturgy are all forms of feedback—significant feedback worthy of consideration by message senders.

Feedback that indicates a message's failure to connect is not, of itself, a problem.  The effective communicator neither resists nor dismisses such feedback from an intended audience.  In evaluating the communications process, a good communicator knows that the important meaning of a message is *not* what the communicator intends; the meaning of a message is the *response* it elicits from the receiver.  If the message results in a response different from that sought by the sender, the communicator assumes that the failure is on the message-sender's part.

In the communications process, listening is as important as transmitting.  Church leaders must develop methods of listening as well as of proclaiming, to listen in order to articulate ideas in a way that communicates feeling as well as content.[14]  There has to be feedback to ascertain the extent to which the message has actually been understood, believed, assimilated and accepted.  As Monica M. McGinley, National Public Relations Director for the Medical Mission Sisters, observes: "The so-called 'silent majority' of the 1970s has been replaced by a new, vocal public, which considers itself a respected and intelligent partner in the communication process.  Feedback is no longer a weak link in the communication chain...it occurs over and over again."[15]

*Communicator, message, audience, code, nonverbals, noise, frame of reference* and *feedback*—all of these components and factors are at work in every communications activity, from the Sunday liturgy to the Sunday bulletin to the Sunday newspaper.  How this communications model can be used to build and maintain parish community is the focus of the next chapters.

# WORKSHOP: Evaluating Your Parish Bulletin

Consider the lowly parish bulletin. We stuff it in our pocket or purse after Sunday Mass and then (theoretically) at home catch up on the latest wedding banns, altar boys (girls?) and pastoral epigrams. What would we do without it? The most underrated form of Church communication, it is often taken for granted and seldom appraised.[16]

In light of the previous discussion on the process of communication, take the past three or four issues of your Sunday bulletin and evaluate its effectiveness according to the eight elements of the communications model:

## • *Communicator:*

Is there a sense of unity to the information presented? Is it clear how all of these parish programs, activities and events are part of the central mission of the parish?

What attitudes are projected by the editor(s) and writer(s): a series of memoranda from the parish CEO? patriarchal, condescending missives from the shepherd to the sheep? a personal soapbox for the venting of the pastor's spleen each week? Or does the material invite response and participation?

What does the bulletin say about the parish leadership: Is it (too) clear what the pastor's agenda is, what the pastor's "issues" are? Or does the bulletin reflect a parish leadership that recognizes the gifts and contributions of the members of the community and enables every parishioner to be part of the life of the parish?

## • *Message:*

What overall message does your bulletin send: one of vitality and community? Or a loose "federation" of activities and programs, a static routine of Masses and bingo?

How does the parish describe itself on the "flag" (the cover logo): "parish"? "church"? "Christian community"? "parish family"? "faith community"? "Catholic Christian community"? "Roman Catholic Church"? Why is this description used? What are you trying to say by using that description? Does the bulletin reflect that description? Does the *parish* reflect that description?

Is it clear in each item what you want your audience to *do* as a result of reading it?

Why is each item in your bulletin worth reading? Is that value clearly articulated in each item?

Are the "five Ws and one H"—Who, What, Where, When, Why and How—that are found in every good news story found in each article in your bulletin?

• *Audience:*

Do the articles give readers a compelling reason to act on the information presented?

Is it clear *how* they should act on the information and *why* they should act?

Do they see how their lives will be richer by their participation in and support of the many ministries of the parish?

In its layout, design and organization, is the bulletin "reader friendly"?

• *Code:*

Do ideas follow in an orderly sequence that is easy to follow?

How much clarity is lost in the use of *jargon*—technical words, phrases and concepts that your readers may not understand and appreciate?

Is the writing crisp, clear and concise?

Is the writing conversational in tone and style? Would you *say* things as they are *written* in the bulletin? Are the words and sentences natural and conversational, or stilted, sterile, flowery, grandiose?

• *Noise:*

Is it time to shoot the mimeograph machine? Should the ditto machine be retired?

When do most people actually read the parish bulletin? Is it the best time and place?

How much "white space" (area not covered with printing) is there in your bulletin?

Is the bulletin top-heavy with type—long paragraphs that go on and on without a break?

Are graphics, illustrations and photographs used to enhance and draw readers into stories—or are they merely used as "decorations?"

• *Nonverbals:*

Every publication has a personality. If you had to describe the *personality* of your parish bulletin in one word, what would that word be:

| | |
|---|---|
| inviting? | authoritarian? |
| interesting? | institutional? |
| personal? | a duty roster? |
| informative? | a bulletin board? |
| lively? | humorless? |
| compelling? | all-business? |
| reflective? | pietistic? |
| witty? | stuffy? |

What does the quality of the printing, paper and typesetting (typing) say about the importance of the parish bulletin in the life of the parish?

Has the editor(s) been careful and constant in spelling, grammar, punctuation and the correct use of titles?

What are the procedures for proofreading the bulletin before it is printed?

Are there sudden shifts from formal language to the use of slang?

• *Feedback:*

Is there any attempt to solicit opinions about the bulletins?

When the bulletin asks for a specific response, do you get it?

How many bulletins are left crumpled in the benches at the end of Mass each Sunday?

Does the parish make any effort to get copies to parishioners who don't come to Mass each weekend? Do any copies find their way into hospitals and nursing homes in your area?

If you purchase a pre-printed bulletin cover, do you have any sense that people read the material on the cover?

• *Frame of Reference:*

Is it clear in each item exactly to whom the item is addressed or intended?

How will the various members of the community "read" each item?

Do bulletin items ever take into consideration attitudes, experiences and viewpoints that are contrary to the objectives of the bulletin's messages? Are such attitudes ever challenged in the pages of the bulletin? Is the bulletin bilingual or trilingual? Why? Why not?

As specific communications strategies and resources are discussed in the next chapters, you may want to make notes of additional ideas to make full use of the message-sending potential of your parish bulletin.

# Notes

1. Stewart L. Tubbs and Sylvia Moss, *Human Communication*, 5th ed. (New York: Random House, 1987), 6.

2. Ibid., 19.

3. Don Hill, "Congruent Communications," *Public Relations Journal*, October 1982, 13.

4. Ibid., 14.

5. Tony Schwartz, *The Responsive Chord* (Garden City, New York: Anchor Press/Doubleday, 1973), 55.

6. Karl Rahner, *Concern for the Church* (New York: Crossroads Press, 1981), 118.

7. Warren Bennis and Burt Nanus, *LEADERS: The Strategies for Taking Charge* (New York: Harper & Row, Publishers, 1985), 107.

8. Bruce E. Gronbeck, Douglas Ehninger, Alan H. Monroe with Kathleen German, *Principles of Speech Communication*, 10th brief ed. (Glenview, Illinois: Scott, Foresman and Company, 1988), 74-76.

9. Ibid., 78.

10. Richard E. Petty and John T. Cacioppo, *Attitudes and Persuasion: Classic and Contemporary Approaches* (Dubuque, Iowa: Wm. C. Brown Company Publishers, 1981), 8.

11. Otis Baskin and Craig Aronoff, *Public Relations: The Profession And The Practice*, 2nd ed. (Dubuque, Iowa: Wm. C. Brown Company Publishers, 1988), 58-59.

12. Schwartz, *Responsive Chord*, 24-25.

13. Roger Ailes with Jon Kraushar, *You Are the Message: Secrets of the Master Communicators* (Homewood, Illinois: Dow Jones-Irwin, 1988), 26.

14. James C. Fenhagen, *Mutual Ministry* (Cambridge, Mass.: Harper & Row, 1977), 116.

15. Monica McGinley, "Megatrends in Religious Public Relations," *Media & Values*, Spring 1984, 12.

16.  Ed Marciniak, "Pray for the Parish Bulletin Editor," *Upturn* (Newsletter of the Association of Chicago Priests), April-May 1987, 10.

# Chapter 2

# The Pastor as Communicator

The pastor of a large suburban parish of some 1200 families, who was ordained in the early 1960s, often says, "You know, I wasn't ordained for this Church." The words are not said with remorse or even sadness, but with wonder at all the changes that have taken place since his ordination; there is a hint of regret that he has not received the needed training for being a pastor in the 1990s.

Many priests, truth be told, share this pastor's sentiments. No, this is not the Church that many of today's priests were ordained to serve. Fewer and fewer of their co-workers in the parish vineyard are brother priests; more and more are good, dedicated and skilled lay men and women and religious. "Father" is no longer the most educated in a parish once made up predominately of peasants and immigrants. Pastors can no longer effectively rule by fiat, but must lead by reason, inspiration and example.

As a communicator, today's pastor must possess not only a facility with words and images but an attitude and vision that is able to see the world from the perspective of the audience. The role of the parish communicator begins with an understanding of the concepts of *identity, image, authority, leadership* and *credibility*.

## Your Identity as 'Parish'

Why does your parish exist?

Why do people belong to your parish? What do they expect from their participation? What *should* they expect from their membership? How do your parish's many activities—everything from worship to education to recreational activities—respond to the Gospel challenge of being *ecclesia*?

These are very basic questions, of course.  But have you ever thought about the answers?  Could you articulate those answers clearly and concisely?  Would the members of your parish council answer as you would?  Would the members of the parish staff?  And how would the people who regularly attend the 10 A.M. Mass answer?  Or the Saturday vigil Mass?  Or parents who send their children to your religious education program?

It is very difficult to communicate anything about your organization unless and until you understand the nature of your organization—its hopes, its goals, its reason for being, its strengths, its weaknesses.  Before Proctor & Gamble launches a new advertising campaign for its new "Mega-Soap," the very first thing they do is to make sure that "Mega-Soap" is a good, reasonably effective, marketable product that people will want to buy.  Similarly, parishes should begin their communication programs by making sure they understand who they are as a parish and what they are all about.  Why does your parish exist?  What makes your parish a unique community within the larger community of your city or town?

Many parishes have developed short "mission statements" that articulate clearly and succinctly their identity as a parish community.  While such mission statements are helpful documents to have for reference, the real benefit in a mission statement is the actual *exercise* of developing and writing such a statement, of bringing the different constituencies of the parish together to discover together exactly what makes them a parish.

A Catholic college, not too long ago, named a new president.  Upon taking office, the president was confronted with a myriad of questions and problems—and for every problem, he received a myriad of suggestions from different segments of the college community as to how to deal with those problems.  What particularly struck the new president was how many of the suggestions were at complete odds with others, indicating very different expectations and visions of the college's reason for being.

So the president initiated a process of developing a mission statement for the college.  The process involved every segment of the college community and took a full year to complete.  The goal was to write a short, concise statement to explain why this particular college was founded and continues to exist.  More than a few professors scratched their mortarboards wondering why it was necessary to write such a statement—after all, the college existed to educate students, did it not?

But in the course of writing the statement, many issues and conflicting points of view surfaced, including the academic emphasis of the college, the role of athletics in student life, the college's vision of itself as primarily a "national" or "regional" school.

The final text of the mission statement that was approved by the Board of Trustees was less than 150 words. But the statement became the starting point for every activity of the college—from writing new admissions brochures to applying for grants.

Such a mission statement puts everybody on the same wavelength. Developing a mission statement, or a series of goals and objectives, can be a particularly good way for a new pastor to begin his ministry in his new parish or to invigorate a long dormant community.

Another excellent way to discover and define your parish identity is to assemble a brochure or guidebook for new parishioners. The effort to explain the various ministries and services of the parish and to identify the persons responsible for each of them will help every person who either contributes material or refers to the guidebook after its publication to understand your parish's character as a unique community of faith.

## Projecting an Image of 'Welcome'

*The Internal Revenue Service. Godiva Chocolates. The President. Brooks Brothers. Cleveland. J.C. Penney. Exxon. Chrysler-Plymouth. The Vatican. Haagen-Dazs Ice Cream. Your bishop.*

Every item on this list triggered a picture of some kind in your mind the instant you read it, didn't it? For some items, the picture was very positive and favorable, while your first picture of others was unfavorable, negative, maybe even hostile. Those first pictures are what communications professionals call *image.*

Many people associate the term "image" with a slick Madison Avenue media campaign. Public images, however, are not just produced by men and women in gray flannel suits. Every public person, product, service and institution projects an image—and everyone connected with such a person or group has a hand in forming that image, whether he or she intends to or not.

An organization's image is a composite of the attitudes and beliefs various "publics" have about an organization (the reason for the plural "publics" will be discussed in Chapter 3). Images are communicated neither directly nor immediately. They are built over time, developed through the cumulative effect of many messages. A parish's image is formed in the mind of parishioners, volunteers, staff and the community at-large not simply through the "official" statements of the Church, but through its activities.[1]

So what is *your* parish's image—how do others see your parish: favorably? negatively? apathetically? Very possibly, it may be all three—some people see the parish as a wonderful, dedicated organization; some might see it as ineffective or narrow-minded or incompetent; others may know absolutely nothing about the parish; a few, perhaps, view the parish with anger or derision. Exactly what do people think of you? Why do people feel the way they do about your parish? What has the parish and its leadership done—or not done—to make people feel the way they do?

Never mind if they're right or wrong in their assessments. Finding excuses and rationalizations for the past is useless; deal first with discovering what people think of your parish and why—and 90 percent of the time you'll find that there is at least some part of their perception that is correct. Assessing your image demands that special kind of honesty that frees you not only to accept the bad news but also motivates you to do something to change it.

For most organizations, images are *not universal*. Images vary from one group to another. One or two images, however, may very well be held by a majority of individuals and groups.

Some images are not entirely of the parish's making. Outside forces can have a powerful impact on a parish's image. One such force is the media. A reporter, for example, may describe a parish's participation in the Birthright organization as part of the Church's "tough anti-abortion stand"; but the parish sees its involvement in such work as a natural part of its "pro-life" commitment and to offering compassionate service to those in need. Yes, the Church opposes abortion. But which of the two "images"—"anti-abortion" or "pro-life"—is the more positive, more inviting, more loving "image"?

The good news is that images are *not permanent*. Images can change—and *be* changed; but to paraphrase Karl Menninger, to change an image, one must, first, accept it.

In many cases, it is not what a person hears or reads but what he/she actually experiences that determines a particular image.[2] The "bad" experiences many people have had with priests and religious have been well-documented. The challenge to today's parishes is to develop a "welcoming spirit," which permeates the entire community, beginning in families and extending to church and neighborhood and community affairs. Rev. Robert J. Hater, Professor of Religious Studies at the University of Dayton, writes that "in a mobile country, where the average person moves once every three years and makes a long distance move once every five years, offering welcome to the newcomer is an important ministry."[3]

Projecting that image of welcome in the parish begins, not with a slick media campaign, but with the many simple and ordinary ways the parish makes contact with the public. Some examples to consider:

- More damage can be done to a parish's image through the telephone than through just about any other medium of communication. This fact takes on added importance when you realize that, often, a newcomer's first contact with your parish community comes in a phone call to the rectory. If you are the pastor or parish secretary who picks up the phone to respond to the "umpteenth" inquiry concerning the Mass schedule, it helps to remember that the caller on the other end wants to be part of the community. Despite your frustration, let that person hear some words of welcome.

  Many parishes have installed answering machines to handle routine calls. While nobody likes talking to a machine, it is better than no answer at all. If your parish decides to employ such a service, do so with care. Too many machines sound like cold-blooded robots:

*ST. PATRICK'S PARISH. MASSES THIS WEEKEND: SATURDAY AT 5 P.M., SUNDAY AT 8, 10 AND 12 NOON. CONFESSIONS HEARD BEFORE MASS OR BY APPOINTMENT.*
—Click.

Makes you want to rush right over, doesn't it?

Now consider the attitude projected in *this* answering-machine response:

*HELLO, AND THANK YOU FOR CALLING ST. PATRICK'S PARISH. OUR PARISH COMMUNITY INVITES YOU TO JOIN US FOR THE EUCHARIST THIS WEEKEND. MASSES ARE CELEBRATED SATURDAY EVENING AT 5 O'CLOCK, AND SUNDAYS AT 8 AND 10 A.M. AND 12 NOON. A PRIEST IS AVAILABLE FOR CONFESSION BEFORE MASS OR BY APPOINTMENT. IF WE CAN BE OF FURTHER ASSISTANCE, PLEASE CALL 000-0000. THANK YOU FOR CALLING.*

Your parish's image is at stake every time the telephone rings.

- The next time you attend Mass at another parish, pick up a copy of their parish bulletin. What does it tell you about that parish community? Is the bulletin just a list of events and schedules? While expensively produced bulletins may look impressive, the content and tone are the keys. Even a bulletin printed on a cheap "ditto" machine can be an extremely effective vehicle for communications and community-building if it conveys a spirit of welcome and of community.

- Some parishes apparently have not gotten the word: the days of the catacombs are over. In many locales, even in tourist areas, the location of the Catholic church is one of the best kept secrets in town. In this regard, Catholics can learn a lesson from our Protestant sisters and brothers. Not only do many advertise on the weekly church pages in local newspapers, many also spread the word of welcome through listings in the yellow pages of the telephone directory, in area information and tourist guides and through directory cards in hotels and visitors' information centers.

- Take a look at the front lawn of your church and the vestibule. What signs of welcome are there? The joke about all the Catholic churches named "St. Bingo" may be more real than pastors would like to think.

- The appearance of your buildings—both internally and externally—contributes to your parish's image. The condition of signs, carpets, paint, landscaping and overall orderliness communicates a great deal about that parish's sense of caring and the spirit of welcome it projects.

- Today they are sometimes called "ministers of hospitality" or "greeters;" they used to be called "ushers." Regardless of their title, they are the first-line of welcome every weekend. The duties of usher may not be as "glamorous" as that of the lector and the extraordinary minister of the Eucharist, but they are no less visible and no less a ministry. The parish's image of welcome begins with them; they should be trained to welcome, to serve, to enable parishioners to feel a part of the life of the parish. It is more than handing out bulletins, passing the collection plate and knowing which lights to turn on and off; it is a matter of attitude and a desire to build community.

- Homiletics and liturgy (while not a principal focus of this book) are primary vehicles of communication in every parish.

In light of this discussion on projecting an image of welcome, consider the *tone* of your preaching and presiding:

As a celebrant, do you project a sense of celebration, of welcome to the congregation, of joy at being with them for this liturgy? Are you aware as you preside at your third or fourth liturgy you celebrate this day or weekend that this is this congregation's *one* and *only* liturgy?

Is your homily typically uplifting and affirming or does it tend to become judgmental, a constant harangue indicting lifestyles and popular values? Does your homily focus on where, in our lives, God is present—or does it usually focus on where he is not?

Overall, is your homily optimistic, without becoming trite and vacuous; or is it pessimistic, dwelling on the pain and suffering of this "vale of tears" with little or no emphasis on the possibilities of resurrection?

Again, while homiletics and liturgy are not singled out for consideration here, they are key communications opportunities. The communication process and principles discussed throughout this book are applicable to the preparation and presentation of liturgies and homilies.

Many studies of the phenomenal growth of Fundamentalist churches and sects in the United States document the fact that many people join these churches because of their emphasis on community and hospitality.[4] One former Catholic, a young woman who is now a member of fundamentalist congregation, explained: "I searched for community in the Catholic Church, but never felt welcome. I wondered if people appreciated my efforts (as a volunteer at parish activities and as service minister). With few activities for young people, I joined adult groups, but was out of place. I learned little about the Bible. Now my new church community supports and welcomes me, while I learn Jesus' teachings and the message of his church."[5]

And most parish ministers serving in most Catholic parishes know someone like this woman.

# The Authority of Inspiration

The Notre Dame Study of Catholic Parish Life quantified many of the changes that have taken place, first, since World War II and then as a result of the Second Vatican Council. Researchers have concluded what many have suspected, and maybe even feared: today's Catholic is a much different participant in the life of the Church than his/her parents and grandparents:

An increasingly educated and moderately prosperous group, more of the laity now have the skills required for parish leadership and the feeling that they, not the clergy and bishops alone, are the Church. As the country has moved from the production line to high-tech and service industries, and succeeding generations of Catholics have moved from blue collar to white collar and professional occupations, many are finding their everyday work settings less hierarchical; they share responsibility; authority resides in the group, not the top leader. When work life is thus arranged, it seems to them natural to transfer that model to the parish setting. Social and economic realities take the laity a long way from "Father knows best."[6]

Psychologist Eugene Kennedy of the University of Chicago notes in his book *Tomorrow's Catholics, Yesterday's Church:*

"(People) come to the Church with definite expectations and dreams. Their lives are spiritually and emotionally attuned to the Church as a sacramental source of interpretation and transmission of meaning, tradition, and teaching, as well as an agent for pastoral support and consolation. We are not talking about the unobservant, Catholics in name only, nor are we talking about the actively rebellious, standing in the front ranks of those described as rebellious."[7]

For today's "core" Catholics, their faith is a way of life. They have enough to do managing the problems of their everyday existence. They are absorbed not by the Church's institutional issues but by the demands of the simplest virtues—faith, hope and love—that are still literally and symbolically the breath of their days. They look to the Church for support in carrying out their responsibilities to their families and to calibrate their moral and ethical compasses. They expect that the Church can speak to them with wisdom and encouragement of the great moral issues of the day. They expect the Church will comprehend tragedy and joy and that it will stand with them in both.[8]

For centuries the Church has fought to assert its "authority" in human and moral affairs. It was successful in doing so, for the most part, large, because the Church possessed a monopoly on "authority" by virtue of its economic and educational control. Even though these monopolies have long been broken, the Church still possesses an authority all of its own: the authority of *inspiration.* The authority the Church possesses today comes not from the power to enforce but from its ability to inspire. Michael Gallagher articulated the authority of today's Church quite eloquently in a reflection for *Notre Dame Magazine*:

> The only real authority is the authority whose warrant goes beyond the frontier and penetrates the interior of the continent. The only real church authority is an authority you and I recognize as compelling when no one else will ever know the difference. Nor does our refusing to agree with it, or even obey it on occasion, lessen its validity. To disagree with or to disobey authority is not the same as rejecting authority . . .

> The Church has authority over me, an authority I acknowledge, that I could probably not shake even if I tried. The Church has authority over me because of Flannery O'Connor, Gordon Zahn, Dorothy Day, Ignatius Loyola, Francis Xavier, Isaac Jogues, Jean de Brébeuf, Helder Camara, Charles Clement, John XXIII, Raymond Hunthausen, Teresa of Avila, Teresa of Calcutta, Daniel Berrigan, Ita Ford, Jean Donovan, Dorothy Kazel, Maura Clarke and Oscar Romero.

> And because of Sister Mary and Sister Vincent de Paul, who taught me at St. Philomena's School in East Cleveland more than 20 years ago; because of Sister Lucy, who works tirelessly for the neglected elderly in my parish; because of Pat Henderson, who helps Sister Lucy while cheerfully caring for her own aged mother and aunt; because of the Brazilian priests, bishops and seminarians who converged a decade ago to protect mourners of a murdered student activist from the soldiers ready to attack them outside of a São Paulo Church.

The Church has authority over me because all these people and many more *inspire* me. Because I recognize the Spirit at work within the church and feel the compunction to pay heed.[9]

# Leader vs. Manager

Our Catholic theology frequently speaks of ministry in terms of *power:* the power to forgive sins, the power to change bread and wine into the body and blood of Christ, the power to ordain men to the priesthood. But in communications, authentic power is *the basic energy to initiate and sustain action, translating intention into reality.*[10]

Historically, many leaders have controlled rather than organized, administered repression rather than expression, and held their followers in arrestment rather than in evolution.[11] Warren Bennis and Burt Nanus, in their study, *Leaders: The Strategies for Taking Charge,* note that "the problem with many organizations, and especially ones that are failing, is that they tend to be overmanaged and underled."[12] There is a profound difference between management and leadership, and both are equally important.

To *manage,* sayeth Webster, means to bring about, to accomplish, to have charge of or responsibility for, to conduct; to *lead,* however, means to guide, to influence in direction, course, action, opinion.

To appreciate the distinction between leadership and management, consider the following situation. The pastor and one of the parish's permanent deacons, who serves as liturgist, and the music director meet several times before the Easter Triduum liturgies. Music is selected that both enhances the meaning of the liturgies and can be "handled" by the choir and congregation. Together they study the prayers, readings and rubrics of the Holy Thursday, Good Friday and Easter Vigil services. Then the pastor, who will be the celebrant, rehearses the chants, studies the readings and develops his homilies. The deacon explains the services and rehearses them with the lectors and acolytes. The music director works with the choir and musicians.

At the celebration of each service, the pastor-celebrant becomes the *leader* of the celebration, the deacon and music director are its *managers.* Through his role as leader of the service, the celebrant articulates the meaning and vision of the liturgy; the deacon and music director, through their "managing" of the assistants, musicians and other participants, make that vision a reality for the congregation.

More and more priest-pastors are becoming the leaders of their parishes while the role of manager is being taken over by qualified lay folks—as it should be. The managerial needs of the community should be the responsibility of those who have talents and training in the specific areas of parish life.

The distinctions between *leaders* and *managers* have been concisely catalogued by Professor Abraham Zaleznik in a study for the *Harvard Business Review.* Professor Zaleznik points out the differences as they relate to four areas common to all organizations:

## • *Attitudes toward goals*

LEADERS approach goals from an active rather than a reactive stance, shaping ideas instead of responding to them. Leaders adopt a personal and active attitude toward goals. "The influence a leader exerts in altering moods, evoking images and expectations, and in establishing specific desires and objectives determines the direction an (organization) takes. The net result of this influence is to change the way people think about what is desirable, possible and necessary."[13]

MANAGERS tend to adopt impersonal, if not passive, attitudes toward goals. Managerial goals arise out of necessity rather than desire and are deeply imbedded in the history and culture of the organization.[14] In terms of communications, good managers make clear to the organization's members how and why their work meets the organization's goals articulated by the leadership.

## • *Conceptions of work*

LEADERS seek to develop fresh approaches to longstanding problems and to open issues for fresh options. Where managers seek to limit choices, leaders work in the opposite direction. Focussed on ideas, the leader must project those ideas into images that excite people, and then develop choices that give the projected images substance.[15]

MANAGERS tend to view work as the way to get things done, an enabling process involving some combination of people and ideas interacting to establish strategies and make decisions. "Managers help the process along by a range of skills, including calculating the interests in opposition, staging and timing the surfacing of controversial issues, and reducing tensions."[16]

## • *Relations with others*

LEADERS, concerned with ideas, relate to others in empathetic and intuitive ways. A leader's attention is on what the events and decisions mean to participants.[17]

Primarily concerned with how to get things done, MANAGERS relate to people according to the role they play in a sequence of events or in a decision-making process. This orientation to others as actors in a sequence of events deflects his/her attention away from the substance of people's concerns and toward their roles in a process.[18] The communications challenge to both leaders and managers is to make members of the organization feel a sense of ownership for the vision and a sense of responsibility for their roles in making that vision a reality. Dr. Zaleznik points out the long-term dangers of communicating in "signals" rather than messages:

> A signal has a number of possible implicit positions in it while a message clearly states a position. Signals are inconclusive and subject to reinterpretation should people become upset and angry, while messages involve direct consequence that some people will indeed not like what they hear. The nature of messages heightens emotional response and emotionally makes managers anxious.

> With signals, the question of who wins and who loses often becomes obscured.[19]

## • *Sense of self*

LEADERS are people who feel separate from their environment, including other people. They may work in organizations, but they never "belong" to them. Their sense of who they are does not depend on memberships, work roles or other social indicators of identity.[20]

MANAGERS see themselves as conservators and regulators of an existing order of affairs with which they personally identify and from which they gain rewards. Perpetuating and strengthening institutions enhances a manager's sense of self-worth—he/she "is performing in a role that harmonizes with the ideas of duty and responsibility."[21]

Probably one or two monsignorial Chancery-types came to mind as you reviewed the managers' attributes above, right? But the point is that *both* leaders and managers are needed in the parish:

- the LEADER who articulates the vision, empowers others to make the vision real and supports them with the emotional and physical resources they will need; and

- the MANAGER who possesses the organizational skills and the expertise to get the tasks done and to mobilize the physical resources (human, capital, technological) of the parish to make the vision real. The desire and ability to communicate are essential to the pastor who understands the role of serving as the leader the faith community.

## Credibility: 'The Terms of Priesthood'

Everything discussed to this point comes down to one thing: credibility. All of the above could be carefully and exactingly in place, but without credibility, it is all for nought.

The simple fact is that audiences accept ideas mainly from communicators they trust. Take away a communicator's moral character in the minds of the audience, and the communicator's power evaporates.[22] Rev. Philip J. Murnion, Director of the National Pastoral Life Center, puts it very succinctly:

The priest must recognize that the quality of his own life becomes the terms of his priesthood. Consequently, the conditions of that life must respect his own identity as a sacrament of encounter with God...Parish priests and current seminarians must have the human ability to

# LEADERS vs. MANAGERS

| | The Leader | The Manager |
|---|---|---|
| | Articulates images, expectations and objectives | Goals arise out of necessity to complete tasks. |
| | Active rather than *re*active, shaping ideas rather than responding to them. | |
| | Enables people to change the way they think about what is desirable, possible and necessary. | |
| *Conceptions of Work* | Seeks to develop choices and fresh approaches to problems. | Concerned with limiting choices to best option for completing necessary task. |
| | Projects his/her ideas into images that excite people, then develops choices to give those images substance. | Possesses organizational and strategic skills needed to get things done. |
| | | Views work as an enabling process to determine strategies and make decisions. |
| *Relations with others* | Relates to people in empathetic and intuitive ways. | Relates to people impersonally, to the role they play in getting things done. |
| | Values people and what events and decisions mean to them. | |
| *Sense of self* | May work in organizations, but never "belongs" to them. | Sees himself/herself as a conservator and regulator of the existing order. |
| | Does not depend on memberships, work roles or other social indicators for identity. | Self-worth tied to perpetuating/strengthening the institution. |

**Fig. 2.** LEADERS vs. MANAGERS

learn from the world as they engage people in the sacraments of the church and call them to the possibilities of priestly activity in the world.[23]

The fact that one is ordained is a major asset in terms of credibility. Ordination is a bond, a trust between ministers and the people they serve. Many consider ordination as an "authorization" to do the work of ministry.

(Which raises an important issue in terms of "lay" ministry: Many parishioners will not respond in the same way nor accept a "lay" minister serving them when they expect "Father" to be there for them. This reality has to be confronted by parish communities employing lay men and women—regardless of how well-trained they are—in ministry usually undertaken by the ordained.)

Ordination gives the minister stature in the eyes of parishioners, similar to the stature that exists for the teacher in the eyes of students or for the chief executive officer in the eyes of the company's managers. But this "built-in credibility" is a very fragile thing. Years ago, when the the parish priest was the only one in the community who had an education beyond basic reading and arithmetic, his word was accepted as law. In today's parish, however, Father is not the only one with education, training and experience.

What the pastor does offer parishioners, however, is a new perspective on the world, a view of the world based on faith. The pastor is one of God's human creatures, who also struggles with the same questions that they do; but the pastor brings to the parish Christ's light to illuminate life's darkest passages. Credibility, then, goes to the heart of the pastor's vocation.

The important interconnection of the concepts of identity, image, authority, leadership and credibility in the pastor's role as communicator is illustrated in the story of a local Congregational church which dismissed its pastor. The chairman of the church board was asked why they fired him. "Well," the chairman explained, "he kept telling us we're all going to hell."

Well, what does the new pastor say? he was asked.

"Oh, the new pastor says we're going to hell, too."

So what's the difference?

"The difference is that when the old pastor said it, he sounded like he was glad about it. But when the new pastor says it, he sounds like it's breaking his heart."

# WORKSHOP:
# Developing a Parish Mission Statement

Peter Drucker is considered by many in corporate America as the "father of modern management." He has been a management consultant to many Fortune 500 companies and the author of 23 books, including *The Effective Executive, Managing for Results* and *the New Realities.*

Mr. Drucker, an Episcopalian, has said, "I became interested in management because of my interest in religion and institutions." He sees today's mainline churches having a major management/vision problem:

> One of the basic weaknesses of the mainline liberal Church is that it hasn't maintained the common vision. Spiritual needs within the congregation are not being addressed. The leaders see the Church as dedicated to social causes outside the Church. But the congregation doesn't see it that way. The result is confusion and ineffectiveness. This is the priest's challenge—to maintain that common mission . . .

> Churches have to admit that some causes are not their responsibility, even though people often feel that the Church exists to take care of problems . . . The Church needs to concentrate (its) efforts on one or two areas they can excel in and not feel responsible for every cause. This means making sure the work gets done without trying to take on other tasks that divert their efforts."[24]

Whether one accepts or questions Mr. Drucker's analysis, it does focus on the fundamental questions facing every institution, including the parish: Exactly why does the parish exist? What is it designed to do? What can this parish community do that other groups and similar communities cannot do, and what can this parish community do better than other groups? What should parishioners expect from their membership and participation in their parish?

Many parishes have developed mission statements—short (150 words or so) statements that articulate the answers to the above questions. The *process* of developing such a statement is as important and as beneficial as the finished product: it affords the various constituencies of the parish the opportunity to come together to consider exactly what their parish is about (and what it is *not* about) and their hopes and goals for their life together. If done well, a mission statement can and should be the starting point for every parish program and activity.

A mission statement emerges from the parish's reflection upon the history, environment, values, resources and opportunities that are unique to that congregation—how God has shaped the past of the congregation and how the congregation can fulfill God's purpose today. On the basis of its mission statement and the process of writing it, parish leaders can deal more effectively with the issues and questions affecting the community's life together, as well as make better decisions about the allocation of the parish's resources.

There are a number of ways to approach the writing of a mission statement. Good mission statements are developed through a process similar to the following:

1. Begin with as many people in the parish as you can. The group should reflect as many of the various constituencies of the parish as possible: those involved in music and liturgy, religious education, the parish school, youth ministry, finances, and so on, as well as the parish leadership (pastor, staff and council). Ask each person to list on a single sheet of paper

- their definitions of "church,"
- why they belong to the parish and
- their hopes for and expectations of their parish.

2. A small working group should then take the collected sheets and begin to forge a report document. This first report should include a compendium of what people have said about the parish.

3. From this report and reactions to it, the first draft of a statement can be written. This task should be turned over to a small working group. If at all possible, this group should include someone who has special talents as a writer and editor—a great deal of information will have to be synthesized into short, clear, concise statements.

4. Then begins the long struggle—and *struggle* is key here—of revising and refining the statement by the parish leadership (such as the parish council). It is at this revising and rewriting stage that the parish comes to grips with some hard decisions as to exactly what it is about. If a statement is adopted too soon, with little or no struggle with the issues, then the benefits of the development experience will have been short-circuited. So the working group should neither be discouraged nor frustrated if the parish leadership sends the statement back for re-working several times. Most effective missions tatements that become a strong base for parish ministry will take a parish about a year to develop.

Once a mission statement is adopted, every effort should be made to place the statement before the entire congregation and make everyone in the parish understand the mission statement's role in the life of the parish. Every device from the bulletin to banners should be used to make the mission statement a vehicle for bringing the parish together.

The tension in developing a parish mission statement (and, from it, a set of goals and objectives) is to come up with a statement that is general enough to reflect the diversity of the parish community while, at the same time, articulating the unique character and attributes of the parish and the congregation it serves.

The following are four actual parish mission statements, the first two by Roman Catholic parishes and the last two by Episcopal parishes:

• **Statement 1:**

> *St. John the Evangelist Church is a Christian community. We are a people of God bonded together in faith. Our faith is rooted in the rich tradition of generations and is responsive to the spiritual needs brought about by an everchanging world.*
>
> *We are a large community respectful of young and old, the rich and poor, the liberal and conservative. However, in the midst of this diversity, we strive for unity. We at St. John's challenge our members to be open, forgiving and loving.*
>
> *We are a people of God who come together to nourish our faith. We are inspired through liturgical celebrations which are*

*prayerful and life-giving to make a Christian difference in the world.*

*In this time when peace is threatened, we recommit ourselves to the values of Jesus Christ. We believe that the Spirit of God is calling each and every member of St. John's to witness his/her faith. This responsibility demands a commitment to the truth that Jesus Christ offers hope to every person. It is our mission to bring about the kingdom of God—a kingdom of peace, harmony, justice and love. We are challenged to be involved and to reach out.*

This "statement of purpose" was written by the parish council as a starting point for its plan for the year. The statement articulates the importance of respect, unity, openness, forgiveness and acceptance in the midst of the parish's diversity (do you sense here an element of "struggle" for this parish?). Prayer and spirituality are viewed as central to the parish's reason for being; from that nurturing of faith evolves the responsibility of each member to witness the peace, harmony, justice and love of the Gospel.

* **Statement 2:**

*Holy Trinity Church,*
*as a Roman Catholic parish,*
*is a community of Christians*
*called to bear witness to Jesus Christ and*
*to love the Gospel of Christ in such a way*
*that others are also attracted to a living out*
*of Gospel values.*

*As a Christian community*
*we are dedicated to worship God,*
*to study the truths of the Gospel and*
*to continue the serving love of Jesus Christ*
*to people with whom we share our daily lives.*

*We believe that the Holy Spirit has bestowed*
*on our members*
*the charisms needed for the renewal and building up*
*of the Church.*

*Through these gifts,*
*we share in Christ's life*
*as priest, teacher and shepherd.*

*As a parish community we face these challenges:*

- *the need to continually challenge and invite our people to a deeper sharing in the life of the faith community through personal involvement in the mission and life of the faith community;*

- *the need to reach out to inactive Catholics and to the unchurched living among us and to invite them to membership in our faith community;*

- *the need to provide all our people meaningful opportunities to understand the Gospel truths more deeply in order to help them form their lives from birth till death according to the magisterium (teachings/customs/traditions) of the Church;*

- *the need to be an active part of the community in which we live and to be concerned with the needs of all people;*

- *the need to participate in the mission and activities of the universal Church through our involvement in the local church of the Archdiocese of N., and prayerful support of the Church's world-wide missionary efforts.*

While comprehensive, this statement needs a more concise, sharper focus.  Much too long, the writers seemed more intent on covering all the bases rather than struggling with the hard decisions demanded if realistic priorities and goals are to be set.  Also a problem in this statement is the use of jargon ("charism," "magisterium") and abstract concepts ("mission and life of the faith community," "Christ's life as priest, teacher and shepherd") that mean little to the average parishioner.

## • Statement 3:

*Emmanuel Church is an open church: anyone who is present here, at any time, is a member of our community. We welcome everyone at whatever point a person may be on his or her journey, for as long as each person wishes.*

*We are together as children of God. As in the long history of Christian fellowship, the center of Emmanuel's life is the Sunday liturgy in which we celebrate our life through the Eucharist and the arts.*

*It is our belief that the questions of human meaning for our time are poignantly raised by the arts. An integral part of our mission, therefore, is to use the language of the arts to communicate Christian judgment, resource, faith and hope.*

*We seek to accept the love of Christ for ourselves and our neighbors by aiding programs which help the victims of injustice and oppression, the sick and the troubled, the poor and forgotten.*

*We pray for freedom from all boundaries that separate us from the all-inclusive love of Jesus Christ. We believe that we know Christ in knowing others, serve Christ in serving others, and love Christ in loving others.*

Note the specific emphasis on the arts: through the years, this parish has developed a special ministry to the arts and has strived especially to incorporate the musical and visual arts in its prayer and worship. The "art" dimension is important to this parish community and they say so, but it is placed in a context of openness and welcome to all people. For this parish, their use of the arts in liturgy is designed to inspire them to manifest the love of Christ in their assistance to "the victims of injustice and oppression, the sick and the troubled, the poor and the forgotten." One benefit of this particular mission statement must be an easing of the tensions that usually exist between parish "liturgists" and "artists," who can bring different—and often conflicting—perspectives to their work. By starting with their mission statement, Emmanuel's liturgists and artists can begin their work together with a clearly-articulated shared goal before them.

### • Statement 4:

*St. Margaret's is an Episcopal parish with ecumenical roots, serving those in N. and nearby communities, who wish to participate as members and worship with us.*

*We are called as baptized Christians to be witnesses for Christ, to live our faith boldly and to proclaim the Gospel.*

*We celebrate the glory of Christ through our liturgy: prayer, education, music and family fellowship.*

*Our commitment to Christian life manifests itself by service within and beyond our community.*

This statement contains the hallmarks of a good mission statement: brevity, focus (on the liturgical and prayer life of the community), and an articulation of the parish's spirit of inclusiveness and uniqueness (geographic location, the importance of music and education in its life together).

A good mission statement focuses the energy of a parish community. It can be the starting point for developing parish goals and opportunities for ministry that are

- *specific*, meaning that the parish has focused its outreach on particular human hurts and hopes—for example, ministry to young families or to the homebound elderly or to Spanish-speaking immigrants (depending on such factors as the demographic make-up and geographic location of the parish); and

- *concrete*, referring to the parish's delivering of effective help, hope, and new life in a competent, compassionate, committed and courageous manner (in other words, exactly how the parish is going to make the "specifics" happen).[25]

A final thought from Peter Drucker:

"Nonprofits aim for change. Hospitals seek to change sick people into healthy ones. Schools aim to change students into educated individuals. The Church's aim is to make a difference in the way a parishioner lives, to change the parishioner's values into God's values."[26]

# Notes

1. Otis Baskin and Craig Aronoff, *Public Relations: The Profession and the Practice*, 2nd ed. (Dubuque, Iowa: Wm. C. Brown Publishers, 1988), 63.

2. Ibid., 64.

3. Robert J. Hater, "Fundamentalism and the Parish," *Church*, Winter 1988, 21.

4. Ibid.

5. Ibid.

6. David C. Leege, "Parish Organizations: People's Needs, Parish Services and Leadership," *Notre Dame Study of Catholic Parish Life*, 8 (Notre Dame, Indiana: University of Notre Dame, 1986), 2.

7. Eugene Kennedy, *Tomorrow's Catholic, Yesterday's Church: The Two Cultures of American Catholicism* (New York: Harper & Row Publishers. 1988), 18.

8. Ibid., 19.

9. Michael Gallagher, "Divine Inspiration," *Notre Dame Magazine*, Summer 1987, 30, 32.

10. Warren Bennis and Burt Nanus, *LEADERS: The Strategies for Taking Charge* (New York: Harper & Row Publishers, 1985), 15.

11. Ibid., 16.

12. Ibid.

13. Abraham Zaleznik, "Managers and leaders: Are they different?" *Harvard Business Review*, May-June 1977, 71.

14. Ibid., 70.

15. Ibid., 72.

16. Ibid., 71.

17. Ibid., 73.

18. Ibid.

19. Ibid., 74.

20. Ibid., 74-75.

21. Ibid., 74.

22. Harry Hazel, *The Power of Persuasion* (Kansas City, Missouri: Sheed & Ward, 1989), 18.

23. Philip J. Murnion, "'The Priest in the 1990s: Scenario and Implications," *Church,* Summer 1988, 7.

24. Peter F. Drucker, "Managing Churches (and other Nonprofit Organizations)," *Crossings,* (Newsletter of the Church Divinity School of the Pacific), Special Issue 13, September 1989, 2.

25. Kennon L. Callahan, *Twelve Keys to an Effective Church: Strategic Planning for Mission* (San Francisco: Harper & Row, Publishers, 1983), 1.

26. Drucker, "Managing Churches," 8.

# Chapter 3

# The Parish 'Audience':
# A Community of Communities

Paul's vision of "one bread, one body" notwithstanding, the one big, happy, congregation that gathers around the altar each Sunday is *not* a homogeneous group.

Today's church communities are no longer single culture/one neighborhood parishes, but are as  pluralistic in values and attitudes as is American society as a whole.[1] Rev. Philip J. Murnion, Director of the National Pastoral Life Center, notes some important differences between the Church of today's Catholics and the Church of their parents:

> *Today the Church is less of a self-contained community; now a significant portion of American Catholics measure their lives by their careers.*
>
> *The measure of spirituality is the extent to which it guides a person's understanding of the world and the extent to which it provides a basis of discipline in one's life...*
>
> *Today's American Catholics clearly have a more voluntary approach than their parents to the way and degree they will participate in church life, whether this is a matter of Church teaching, of parish membership, or of the level of participation in parish life.[2]*

Today's parish is *a community of communities,* an assembly of many different value systems, expectations and levels of comprehension and faith development.  The situation confronting the parish communicator is very much like that confronting advertisers. Major advertisers like Proctor & Gamble and McDonald's realized long ago that there is no such person as the "typical American consumer."  So advertisers determine, at the outset of any ad campaign, their product's specific market: the demographics, educational

43

background, income, attitudes and values of those consumers most likely to purchase the product. Commercials are then designed to target that specific market segment. Some messages might be targeted to appeal to working women who manage a home, teenagers, parents-to-be, or middle-aged men. The messages are then placed in publications and in programs where they will have the best chance to be seen or heard by the intended audience: thus, Revlon ads appear in the pages of *Cosmopolitan*, while Black & Decker power tools are advertised on Sunday afternoon football games on television.

Parish communicators face the same challenge. There is no such parishioner as the typical American Catholic. For the most part, today's Catholics participate in the life of their parish on their own terms, based on their own needs, values and expectations.[3]

Keep in mind that audiences are composed of both *individuals*, each person with unique and sometimes unpredictable tastes, needs and wants, and *groups*, who share identifiable and measurable social and cultural traits, beliefs and attitudes. As discussed in Chapter 1, their experiences both as individuals and as members of a number of groups have led to the development of their frames of references. To communicate effectively, pastors must understand what makes their parishioners "tick" both as individuals and as group members—what is important to them, what they value, what motivates and inspires them.

# Message Impact: 'The Parable of the Splashing Stone'

A common mistake among not only pastors but most organizational leaders is the assumption that every message is equally important and vital to every person in the organization. Nothing could be further from the truth. The fact is that very few messages affect *every* member of an organization. Most messages matter only to *some* members of the organization. The *impact* of a message varies in intensity from group to group within an organization.

Consider the "parable of the splashing stone." A youngster is standing on the edge of a clear lake. The water is perfectly still, the surface is like a piece of glass. The youngster picks up a stone and tosses it into the center of the lake. PLOP! At the point where the rock enters the water, there is a splash. The splash causes waves.

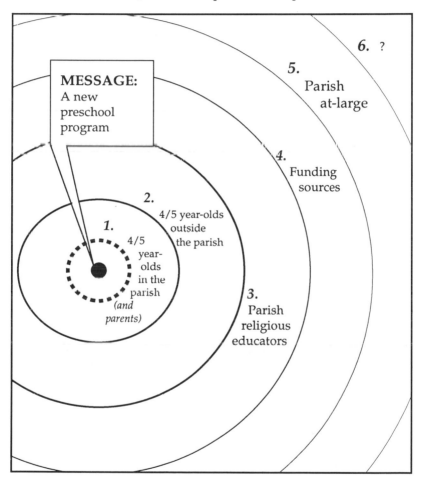

**Fig. 3.** The "parable of the splashing stone" visualizes the varying degrees of intensity and interest a message has on different audiences.

As the waves move farther away from the splash point, they become ripples, which soften to become a gentle movement breaking along the water's surface. From above the lake, the splash is the center of a series of concentric circles moving out to the water's edge.

In the parable, the stone represents the message to be communicated. The message has the most impact on those closest to the "splash." The further away in interest or concern from the splash (and the less intense the wave or ripple), the lesser the impact of the message.

Suppose, for example, your parish decides to begin a religious education program three mornings a week for preschool children, ages four and five. In your "messages" inviting registration for the 20 openings, the principal target audience would obviously be the four- and five-year-olds of the parish and their parents (these parents certainly qualify as the most influential "opinion leaders" in this situation). They are the center of the "splash," the principal audience from which you seek a specific response. Your first and primary communications efforts, then, would be directed to this group.

You might next determine that the second circle is made up of the parents of four- and five-year-olds of neighboring parishes, if you decide to open up registration across parish lines.

The next circle would probably be the religious educators of the parish—the volunteers involved in teaching the other religious education classes and moderating the youth ministries in the parish (notice how the direct impact of this program is lessening as other potential audiences are considered). Although not directly involved in this particular program, they can serve as effective "opinion leaders" because of their identity with and personal investment in religious education.

You might consider potential funding sources as the next outer circle. You may decide that an effort should be directed to communicating with organizations who could support this effort with donations; if so, messages to such groups should make clear to them *why* this religious education program is worthy of *their* support.

Certainly one outer circle or "ripple" is the parish at-large. While they may not be directly affected by this program and have little interest in its details, it is important for the parish community as a whole to see how this program fits into the overall mission of the parish. Every parish activity, from liturgy to education to planting new shrubs on the property should include efforts to communicate to the whole parish community how this particular dimension of parish life is part of the total Gospel-centered mission of the parish (this is where a parish mission statement is particularly helpful). If you have difficulty articulating that relationship clearly and convincingly, maybe the whole program should be reconsidered.

You may find that there are groups beyond the parish community who might be interested to some degree in your message or program. If your preschool program is new and innovative, perhaps religious educators in other parishes around the diocese might be among the "outer ripples" of your "splash."

One direct approach, then, to determine who your principal audiences are is to consider the impact on various constituencies and audiences, based on their interests, goals and values. The "splash" model in communications planning begins with the realization that every message affects different individuals and groups within an organization with different degrees of impact and meaning, that every message does not have the same importance to every member of the organization. As will be discussed in the next chapter on message design and communications planning, the key to reaching a target audience is making clear to that group exactly what impact the message should have on them.

## Same Message, Different Responses

As discussed in Chapter 1, every audience "filters" messages they see and hear through their special "frames of reference"—that composite of the beliefs, attitudes and perceptions they hold as individuals and as members of groups. All messages are filtered through their frames of reference as the audience evaluates and ascribes meaning to them.

While different theories have been forwarded regarding attitude formulation and change, communications research has found some basic principles about the role beliefs, attitudes and perceptions figure in the communications process:

- People organize stimuli according to different schemes and expectations—they attribute cause and effect uniquely. After stimuli are selectively perceived and organized, they are selectively interpreted as well. Personal interpretations are based on the perceiver's past experiences, assumptions about human behavior, knowledge of other's circumstances, present moods, wants, desires and expectations.[4]

- The more an individual is personally involved in his/her beliefs, the harder it is to change them by information or argument.

- People tend to take in messages that affirm their belief and attitude systems; for example, advertising studies show that most people read the ads for products they already own.[5]

- The persuasive effects of mass communication have been found to be mainly *reinforcing*; that is, the views already held by the audience were buttressed or reinforced. Conversions are rare, and many "converts" admit to being dissatisfied with the previous opinion *before* being exposed to the persuasive message.[6]

- Mass communications *is* extremely effective in creating opinion on new issues, or issues on which neither the individual nor the group has an opinion. An example of this phenomenon: the emergence of the ecological and environmental issues of the 1960s.[7]

- Peer groups exert strong pressure to protect their norms from the threat of persuasion. Within the groups to which we belong, there are certain people—opinion leaders—who have a particularly strong influence on the decisions we make.[8] Some advertising industry accounts show, for example, that up to 80 percent of all consumer choices result from personal recommendations.[9]

- People seldom set out to change their attitudes; rather, they usually are exposed to situations and information that cause them to think and feel differently about some object or issue.[10]

- As a group, the hardest to persuade are listeners who possess high self-esteem, are well educated and know that complex issues demand complicated solutions.[11]

- Knowledge is *not* the same thing as a favorable attitude. Communication is often assumed to be successful once the public obtains knowledge about the subject in question. A high degree of awareness is not necessarily an indication that the goal of the message will be realized.[12]

- When the opposition of people cannot be overcome, their resistance might be neutralized so as not to discourage or alienate others. Getting such resistance out into the open, assuring them that their status is not threatened, displaying empathy for their position and encouraging their participation in modifying the new idea can effectively neutralize (if not overcome) opposition.[13]

Knowing and understanding an intended audience's system of beliefs, attitudes and perceptions is vitally important if the message is to be received and understood as the sender intends.

## The 'Twelve Tribes' of the Parish

Take a look at your own parish. You can readily identify certain "groups" of people who share beliefs, perceptions and attitudes that differ from other groups. In many parishes, for example, the "regulars" at the various weekend liturgies are distinct congregations—the group that gathers for the Saturday night folk Mass operates with many different attitudes and beliefs than the older, more traditional communicants who attend the 8 A.M. Mass every Sunday morning.

Any attempt at sociological typography is risky. No grouping system will be perfectly inclusive of every member of an organization; nor can such groupings be considered mutually exclusive—

## The 12 Tribes of the Parish Community

- *Children*

Pre-schoolers. Curious, imaginative. Respond to unambiguous stories of good and evil.

- *The Literalists*

Elementary and middle-school children and adults who take a fundamentalist approach to faith. Understand cause-and-effect relationships: good is re-warded, evil is punished. God is viewed as a stern but just Parent.

- *The Searchers*

Older teenagers and young adults. Stage of transition and struggle.

- *The Survivors*

The poor and neediest of the parish, struggling to make ends meet.
*Also:* The "Ouch People" — those whose temporary presence in the parish seeks comfort and consolation in their time of hurt and loss.

- *The Belongers*

The *middle* middle-class who strive to "fit in." Good workers (but not leaders). Low tolerance for conflict and ambiguity; embarrassed by open emotionalism and sensuality. Prefer the status-quo: value patriotism, home and family, church and loyalty to nation and job.

- *The Traditionalists*

Usually found among the seniors in the parish. View of the Church centered on order, structure and authority. Long for the pre-Conciliar Church of their childhoods.

- *The* Outer-*directed*

Driven by financial success, prestige and security. Include achievers and those who emulate them.

- *The* Inner-*directed*

Driven by "internal" values: faith that challenges, concerns over the environment and nature, aware of the unity of humankind. Include "experientials" and the societally conscious.

- *The* Sectarians

Vision of the Church as a small band of disciples rather than an institution for the "masses." Include CatholicWorkers and justice and peace activists (on the "left") and charismatics (on the "right").

- *The Intimates*

Vision of the Church as family. Value intimacy through renewal. Include the communities of the weekend renewal programs.

- *The Associates*

Identify with the Church through memberships and participation in parish-sponsored organizations and services: school, youth groups, social service programs, etc.

- *The Pilgrim People*

Grounded in God and the kingdom of God. Action is always linked to belief; the past is always linked to the future. An *adult* view of the Church, where lay adults are treated and respected as adults.

**Fig. 4.** The 12 Tribes of the Parish Community.

some members of an organization will invariably be "classifiable" in more than one category.

With those disclaimers in mind, what follows are 12 groups or "tribes" that most pastors can identify within their parish communities. Based on current studies of lifestyles, values and faith development as well as recent surveys of American Catholics' expectations of their parishes, each of these "tribes" possesses unique belief systems, attitudes and perceptions that have important consequences for parish communications efforts.

1. *Children.* Preschool age children bring to the congregation their curiosity, their energy, their imaginations and their special "wonder" that allows them to move freely back and forth across boundaries that they only later will sort out as dividing the conscious and the unconscious, fantasy and reality.[14] Children grasp stories that present the power of good and evil in unambiguous fashion.[15] To communicate with children, establishing trust and creating a bond based on caring and affection are the critical ingredients.[16] Simplicity and clarity are the essential characteristics for any activity in which adults wish to engage children.[17]

2. *The literalists.* There may be two groups of "literalists" in a parish: children of elementary and middle-school age and adults with a fundamentalist approach to faith. Literalists understand cause-and-effect relationships and, accordingly, create systems of classifications. God is seen as a stern but just and fair parent who rewards good and punishes evil.[18]

Messages that affirm this view of the cosmos—that good actions are rewarded and evil is punished—have the best chance of connecting with the literalists. The God they know is the God of power, authority and judgment. The pastoral as well as the communications challenge is to help the literalists recognize a loving God present in the complicated, "gray" world we live in.

3. *The searchers.* The "searchers" are older teenagers and young adults [median age: 21] who are at a stage of transition in their lives: between the value system of parents and elders and staking out their own place in the world on their own terms. It is a time of confusion, contradictions, uncertainties and excesses; but it is also a time of inventiveness, energy and enthusiasm.[19] Searchers are most

receptive to messages that affirm and support their struggle and invite them to take proprietorship for some dimension of their lives in the Church on their terms.

4. *The survivors.* "Survivors" are the poorest and neediest among us. Many are old (the median age is 66), ill and poorly-educated. Not surprisingly, many survivors tend to be despairing, depressed, withdrawn, distrustful, rebellious about their situation, lacking in self-confidence, and finding little satisfaction in any aspect of their lives. Their focus is on the elemental needs of survival and security; the aim is not so much to get ahead as not to slip backward.[20]

Some survivors have been trapped in the culture of poverty all their lives, while a growing number, through bad luck, a lack of enterprise or the onslaught of old age or catastrophic illness, slip into the survivor lifestyle. Survivors live not only in inner-city slums and ghettos but in aging frame houses of small towns and on the porches and shuttered rooms of old folks' homes.[21]

Younger "survivors" seek not merely to survive but, if possible, to move ahead to a better life.[22] Getting and holding a job is a constant problem. Survivors include the impoverished family (often headed by a young single parent) struggling to keep going on minimal wages. Another group of "survivors" are the most recent immigrant trying to make a go of it in a new world.[23]

Also among the survivors are those one pastor calls the "ouch people": people who come and go (whose presence in the parish might be temporary, either by choice or necessity), who seek comfort and consolation at a time of hurt in their lives, such as illness, trauma or loss.

Traditional, conservative and conventional, survivors present a special pastoral challenge to the rest of the parish community. Messages that affirm their self-worth, their dignity and their ability to make a contribution to the common life of the parish—without patronizing them—are essential to making contact with them. An important "nonverbal" must be to convey that the Church understands their plight and does not diminish its seriousness, and that the Church cares for them and about them. Their presence confronts the parish with the Gospel mandate: to feed the hungry, to clothe

the naked, to care for the sick, to give comfort to the imprisoned and afflicted. To welcome strangers.

5. *The belongers.* Belongers, the *middle* middle-class, are driven to "fit in." Overall, they form a large, aging group, a bit removed from the center of action, and tend strongly towards traditional attitudes: traditional, conforming, conservative, "moral," nonexperimental, family-oriented.[24] Some sociological studies have determined that people who fit the lifestyle-pattern of belongers make up more than a third of the U.S. adult population: about 95 percent are white; most are middle-aged or older and have middle-incomes and middle-levels of education, and tend to live in small towns and the open country, shunning the big city.[25]

Belongers prefer the status quo if not the ways of yesteryear: patriotism, home and family, church and loyalty to nation, job and old associations are most important to them. They have the highest confidence in elected officials, the military and mainline institutions.[26] Belongers see safety in numbers. Relationships and associations with others tend to be quite formalized. Open emotionalism and sensuality are embarrassing to them.[27] Central to their sense of identity and worth is the approval and affirmation of significant others.[28]

Though not typically innovative leaders, individual belongers often constitute the most consistent corps of church workers. A sense of harmony and conflict-free connectedness with the parish community is important to them. Conflict and controversy which threaten the ideal of community are especially disturbing and threatening to them.[29]

Belongers have difficulty in relating their faith to social, economic and political structures—analytic approaches to religious experience and to the central symbols of faith may be uninteresting or threatening to them.[30] When confronted with pastoral leadership who insist upon critical and analytical approaches to matters of faith, they may respond in ways which seem anti-intellectual, oriented to emotion and experience, and defensively conventional.[31]

Parish communicators should realize, first, that tolerance for ambiguity is low among belongers. Belongers prefer to follow than to lead, to stick with the tried and true, to trust the system to award "virtue," and to accept the lower common denominator to avoid hostility. "Should," "ought" and "obedience" are important concepts to belongers.[32] The most effective messages are those that present challenges as a logical extension of the belongers' conventional, fair and uncomplicated belief system.

6. *The traditionalists.* These parishioners (most, as one would expect, are found among the seniors in the parish) seek a return to the past. This may take the form of proposing a return to the Baltimore Catechism, the "old" Latin Mass, the pious devotions of the past and earlier forms of church discipline.[33] Their view of church is centered on order, specifically in the leadership of the clergy. They respond to the clarity of such a structure, where the lines of authority are clearly outlined. They shun the ambiguities of Scripture studies, parish councils and sisters who do not wear religious garb.[34] While the belongers in the parish will go along with change (however reluctantly) that the entire Church experiences together, the traditionalists are more adamant that the Church in which they were born and raised is in no need of change. The traditionalists in the parish will most readily respond to messages that connect with the pre-Conciliar concepts of centralization and clerical authority, messages that are clearly defined and leave no room for doubt or vagueness.

7. *The outer-directed.* The "outer-directed" are driven by tangibles like financial success, prestige and security. The visible, the tangible and the materialistic are the yardsticks for measuring success. Control and measurement dominate their lives. They conduct themselves according to what they think others will think, and respond to signals from others.

Some outer-directed individuals are *emulators*, striving to "make it." They work very hard to "move up" the social ladder, but their lack of education, wealth, and social standing will often hold them back.[35] Their blind upward striving seems to force many into deliberately misleading others, such as through conspicuous consumption, following the voguish fashion and spending for only what shows.[36] Sadly, emulators (median age: 27) have a very poor self-image, experience a great deal of rejection and develop a pervasive sense of anger, a distrust of authority figures, and have little faith that "the system" will give them a break.[37]

*Achievers*, middle-aged, prosperous and self-assured, are the builders and leaders of the American dream. Achievers, perhaps up to one-fourth of the American adult population, include the gifted, the hard-working, the self-reliant and the successful. To some, achievers typify the stereotype of the wealthy, successful American; to social critics, achievers represent the establishment.[38] Staunchly Republican and conservative, achievers abhor radical change and support the status quo—after all, much of the "status quo" is of their making. They prefer the social standards of the 1930s, '40s and '50s, the decades when most achievers were growing up.[39]

Many achievers are looked to as opinion leaders in the parish (and many are very much aware of their status as such). They respond to decisiveness and well-planned calls to action for specific, attainable goals. The most effective communications approach with achievers is direct, to-the-point, and personal, acknowledging their success and leadership position and appealing to their faith in the system to make things "work" for everyone.

The challenge in ministering to the outer-directed is to appeal to their basic sense of right and wrong and of fair play to help them see that the "system" may not work for everyone, and how such issues are related to the Gospel.

8. *The inner-directed.* As the name indicates, the "inner-directed" are driven by internal values. Self-reliance and inner growth are most important to them.

Most inner-directed adults were raised in outer-directed (especially achiever) families. But at some point in their lives, they determined that "outer-directedness" was not the way to live a lifetime.[40] They see life as a journey, not a goal. The process of discovering is as important as the discovery itself.

Sociologists identify two inner-directed lifestyles:

*Experientials* seek direct, vivid experience with people, events and ideas.[41] Although well off financially, they are not centrally concerned with money, preferring a relatively simple lifestyle. Their confidence in organizational leaders is consistently less than average.[42] Liberal in politics and morality, experientials (median age: 27) are happy, self-assured, well-adjusted people with faith in the trustworthiness of others and great assurance that they are on top of things. Experientials are concerned with a broad range of issues—from the mystical to social activism—and manifest that concern in their participation in those issues.[44]

*The societally conscious,* successful, influential and mature (median age: 39), are the inner-directed equivalent of the outer-directed achievers, but with fundamental differences in attitudes and beliefs: that humanity should live in harmony with nature and not try to dominate it; that nature has its own wisdom; that small is usually beautiful; that the "non-material" is somehow "higher" than the "material"; that each person can and should help remedy societal problems; that simplicity may be the most powerful lifestyle of the future.[44]

Sophisticated, politically effective and extremely well educated and informed, the societally conscious is a rapidly growing segment. Aggressively confrontational, assured of the integrity of their beliefs, they have arrived at positions of influence in their jobs and communities. In the corporate arena they have spearheaded consumer issues and have powered attacks on corporate practices ranging from investment policies to product safety to more diverse representation on corporate boards.[45] Generally speaking, they are self-confident, independent and believe "the system," both economic and social, needs an overhaul.[46]

The inner-directed have a strong sense of selfhood. Many have had to struggle, to a significant degree, with those external authorities—both personal and institutional—that guide, constrain and support one in growth toward adulthood.[47] Many have returned to active church participation now that they are married and have children of their own, after being away from the Church when they were "searchers" or "emulators." The inner-directed value faith to the degree it supports and expresses their sense of selfhood. Faith can also constitute a source of accountability and directive for one's selfhood.[48]

The inner-directed respond to a different kind of religious leadership than do belongers and traditionalists. While the latter are comfortable with the "mystery" dimensions of faith, the former seek a faith that is both reasoned and reasoning. They enjoy the struggle of making sense of a particular text or tradition of the Church.[49] In other words, the inner-directed of the parish respond to a presentation of faith that is challenging and that integrates the Gospel with the real joys and pains of life.

9. *The sectarians.* The "sectarians" in the parish have concluded that the Church can no longer be a church for the masses but must inevitably be a relatively small band of the elect. The members of the Church are the special disciples of the Lord, giving testimony to the meaning of the Gospel in their lives. That testimony is given usually in one of two ways: sectarians on the "left" express their view of church in symbolic, prophetic actions (demonstrations, fasts, petition-drives, etc.) to call the world to peace and justice; sectarians on the "right" express their church view in testimony or praise rather than in testimony of prophecy.[50] "Left" sectarians are members of the Catholic Worker Movement and Catholic peace and justice organizations, while "right" sectarians are members of the charismatic renewal movements. To sectarians, interior renewal is key: They see the Church as a place of support and acceptance where they can develop their own deep, personal relationship with God and the countercultural claims of discipleship.[51]

10. *The intimates.* This is the community of the encounter weekend, groups like marriage encounter, teen ncounter and similar renewal programs that focus primarily on the emotional relationships among the participants.[52] The "intimates" in a parish seek to break through the feelings of alienation and anonymity that are inherent to contemporary urban culture in order to accept and welcome people. Personal contact, knowing everyone's name, feeling close to God and to one another are important.[53] "Intimates" are reluctant to let teachings divide the Church "family." They respond to messages that appeal to such emotions as love, family and forgiveness.

11. *The associates.* Associates identify their parish "membership" with a specific parish activity in which they participate or organization to which they belong. "Association" is a growing phenomenon in large parishes that offer a number of services and programs in which non-Catholics participate: schools, housing programs, social service programs, senior citizen centers, and the like. While not members of the faith community, associates are connected to the parish through these programs and activities. Any

message affecting their particular association, obviously, will be important to them; the overall pastoral challenge is to make them realize and appreciate how their "association" is part of the total life and mission of the parish.

12. *The pilgrim people.* These people are priceless and all too rare. They have integrated into their lives the decisiveness of outer-direction with the penetration and reflective nature of inner-direction. Psychologically mature, they have an unusual ability to weigh consequences, to consider subtlety along with flamboyance, to see the small within the large and the potential within what has gone wrong.[54] The pilgrim people adapt easily to most conventions and mores but are more powerfully mission-oriented about those things they feel strongly.

The pilgrim people have "decentralized" the importance of self. The "I" is no longer the prime reference point from which the knowing and valuing of faith is carried out; there is, instead, a new quality of participation and grounding in God. This kind of transformation of values gives rise to strategies of nonviolent opposition to entrenched evil in hearts and societies, to transform present social conditions in the direction of God's commonwealth of love and justice, to see one's enemies as God's children who must be loved radically and redemptively.[55]

The comparatively few genuine pilgrim people are able to lead when action is required and able to follow when that seems appropriate. They are quick with laughter and generous with tears. They have found ways to meld work and play and combine close relationships with people with the drive to accomplish (rather than visibly achieve).[56] While they continue to be finite creatures with blind spots, inconsistencies and distorted capacities for relatedness to others, the rare number of individuals at this stage of faith constitute both transforming and critically challenging presences in the parish.[57]

They embody the ideal of parish community. Action is always linked to belief.[58] A high premium is placed on respecting tradition—not the traditionalist's yearning to return to a moment frozen in time, but the tradition of the Church grounded in Scripture and the early Fathers of the Church. The past is always linked with the future, building structures for participation and action on a strong theological foundation.[59] The pilgrim people take an *adult* view of the Church, where lay adults are treated and respected as adults.[60] Grounded in God, they live, in quiet or in public ways, as though the kingdom of God were already a realized fact among us.[61]

Again, the temptation is to start classifying and sorting parishioners according to the "twelve tribes" presented here. That is not the purpose of presenting these models; rather, these models might serve as a set of lenses through which to study the parish both as a community of individuals and as a community of communities, to help pastors and parish communicators understand the beliefs, attitudes and perceptions that are the net result of their experiences. By realizing "where they're coming from," parish communicators can more effectively present to them the joys, the hopes and the challenges of the Gospel, in obtaining their participation in the total life of the parish in which those joys, hopes and challenges are experienced.

Remember, too, that people grow and mature, that in their life's journey they will travel through more than one, perhaps several, of these groups.

A final thought: A common element in all of the great movements of human history—from Christianity to civil rights—has been communication between seemingly opposite lifestyles, classes and social groupings.[62] Through intelligent communication planning and execution, the parish can be the place to make such miracles happen again and again.

## *WORKSHOP:*
# A Case Study in Effective Church Advertising

Consider, for a moment, some of the projects, programs and activities you have asked your parishioners to be a part of. Look back at the "messages" you sent to get them involved:

- Did the target audience—the people most likely to respond—realize you were talking to *them*?
- Did the message "travel" through a channel that would reach that target group?
- Did the message give them a compelling reason to participate?
- Did the message counter any objections they might have to participating?
- Did the message facilitate their ability to respond?

Parish communicators often envision one "mass" (no pun intended) parish audience and address all messages to that "mass." But "mass-targeted" messages are often ignored by the contemporary parishioner who, like most Americans, does not want to be considered just part of the "masses." John O'Toole, in his book, *The Trouble with Advertising . . .* , writes about the phenomenon he calls "the Revolution of the Individual": "Americans have been telling communications researchers that 'I'm not part of the crowd, I'm a person. Pay some attention to me and what I need. Or else.' "[63]

That attitude is encountered by churches as well as toothpaste manufacturers. Many parishes have either lost membership or are serving only a fraction of those who claim membership because parish ministers have not been able to bring themselves to deal with such attitudes.

One of the most successful religious communications campaigns in recent memory to creatively confront the "Revolution of the Individual" has been the Episcopal Ad Project. The project began in 1975 when the Rev. George Martin became the rector of St. Luke's Episcopal Church in Minneapolis. "The church had lost its punch," he recalls. "There was lots of gray hair, and I was doing 20-plus funerals a year. The funerals way out-numbered the baptisms."[64]

The Rev. Mr. Martin realized that going door-to-door in a highly unchurched area would not have paid off much in increased attendance. 65 to 70 percent of the residents in Minneapolis claim a church affiliation, and the rector was realistically trying to reach the relatively small fraction of the remainder who would be attracted to the Episcopal Church.[65]

With the help of Ted McElligott of the award-winning advertising agency of Fallon McElligott (and the son and son-in-law of Episcopal clergy), the rector and copywriter came up with a series of humorous, thought-provoking newspaper ads "to make people open up their mental boxes. This is the first step in opening up the possibility of regular church attendance," Mr. McElligott explains.[66]

The advertising "brought in a steady, small stream of people," the Rev. Mr. Martin says, "never an avalanche." But by the time he left St. Luke's after 11 years of ministry and seven years of advertising, attendance was up 30 percent, and the average age of the congregation had dropped from 55 to 40.[67] On most week nights the church is bustling with everything from exercise classes to Alcoholics Anonymous. Now baptisms outnumber funerals, and the ads—once disdained as undignified by some of the church's hierarchy—are being distributed by some 750 Episcopal churches across the United States.[68] Remember (as noted in Chapter 2): images can be changed, but not overnight.

The Episcopal Ad Project's creations have been effective because, unlike many church ventures into advertising, the message-senders knew exactly who they were trying to reach and the channels to reach them. Humorous and witty, each ad is targeted to confront the attitudes and "open the mental boxes" of a specific audience. Each ad is a combination of a traditional religious image or symbol with a contemporary "spin."

Like any effective advertisement, the Martin-McElligott collaborations personalize a need felt by potential "customers" ("We don't sell cosmetics, we sell hope," as one makeup tycoon puts it).[69] For example:

# Will it take six strong men to bring you back into the church?

The Episcopal Church welcomes you no matter what condition you're in, but we'd really prefer to see you breathing. Come join us in the love, worship and fellowship of Jesus Christ this Sunday.
**The Episcopal Church**

**Fig. 5.** "Will it take six strong men to bring you back into the church?" The Episcopal Ad project.

# Do your kids think Genesis is Phil Collins' old band?

If your children don't know Bible stories from rock lyrics, maybe it's time you introduce them to the word of God. This Sunday, come join us in the Episcopal Church.

**The Episcopal Church**

**Fig. 6.** "Genesis." The Episcopal Ad Project.

# Contrary to popular belief, God welcomes singles, too.

When you come to the Episcopal Church, you'll only come alone once. After that, we consider you family. Come join us this Sunday in the love and fellowship of Jesus Christ.

**The Episcopal Church**

**Fig. 7.** "God welcomes singles, too."  The Episcopal Ad Project.

# Without God, it's a vicious circle.

In a world too often ruled by war, hunger, disease and inhumanity, The Episcopal Church believes there is hope. Join us and grow in the faith and fellowship of Jesus Christ.
**The Episcopal Church**

**Fig. 8.** "A vicious circle." The Episcopal Ad Project.

- The ad "Will it take six strong men to bring you back into the church?" is designed to speak to people who have gotten out of the habit of attending church regularly, except to mark life's milestones.

- Ads such as "Do your kids think Genesis is Phil Collins' old band?" are targeted to parents. Statistics indicate that young adults who have been away from the Church return to active church participation once they become parents.[71] Families return because parents believe that the Church can provide their children the moral and ethical foundation they received from the Church when they were growing up.

- The message "Contrary to popular belief, God welcomes singles, too," confronts the feeling of many single persons who feel out of place in the Church.

- Ads like "Without God, it's a vicious circle" speak to busy, ambitious professional businessmen and women who find themselves caught up in the stress of the "fast track." The messages speak to their need, however sublimated, to find meaning and purpose in their lives.

Note, too, that these ads not only have targeted specific audiences but have zeroed in on a single, clear message. Trying to get the most out of their advertising dollar, institutions often try to get as many words, images and ideas into the ad space and time they have purchased. The main message is often lost in a sea of words or type. Ads often look like they have been assembled by a committee with several agendas before it.

The value of St. Luke's access to professional help in developing these ads cannot be overstated. Religious work can be highly rewarding for advertising agencies. Agencies relish religious work precisely because of the strong emotions connected with the subject; religion, after all, is far more fertile material for creative advertising than soap or cereal. The nature of the subject matter lends itself to the kind of striking, conspicuous work than wins awards and establishes reputations for creativity.[71] Mr. McElligott advises non-profits seeking advertising help to contact local agencies whose work is outstanding. "Many agencies look at non-profit accounts as a challenge. They may be willing."[72] Even if the parish has to pay for such services, the extra expense may be worth it in order to protect the parish's already considerable investment in purchasing the advertising space (or time) for the campaign.

There is, of course, one other important factor that is critical to the future success of any advertising campaign, regardless of the product or service or institution:

You have to be able to *deliver* the product you promise.

# Notes

1. David C. Leege and Thomas A. Trozzolo, "Participation is Catholic Parish Life: Religious Rites and Parish Activities in the 1980s," *Notre Dame Study of Catholic Parish Life,* 3 (Notre Dame, Indiana: University of Notre Dame, 1985), 1.

2. Philip J. Murnion, "The Community Called Parish," *Church,* Winter 1985, 8, 9.

3. Eugene Kennedy, *Tomorrow's Catholic, Yesterday's Church: The Two Cultures of American Catholicism* (New York: Harper & Row Publishers. 1988), 21.

4. Stewart L. Tubbs and Sylvia Moss, *Human Communications,* 5th ed. (New York: Random House, 1987), 39.

5. Tony Schwartz, *The Responsive Chord* (Garden City, New York: Anchor/Doubleday, 1973), 92.

6. Phillip K. Tompkins, *Communication as Action: An Introduction to Rhetoric and Communication* (Belmont, California: Wadsworth Publishing Company, 1982). 230-231.

7. Ibid.

8. Tubbs and Moss, *Human Communication,* 373.

9. "Advertising: Try a Word of Mouth Program," *Communication Briefings,* August 1988, 4.

10. Richard E. Petty and John T. Cacioppo, *Attitudes and Persuasion: Classic and Contemporary Approaches* (Dubuque, Iowa: Wm. C. Brown Company Publishers, 1981), 56.

11.  Harry Hazel, *The Power of Persuasion* (Kansas City, Missouri: Sheed & Ward, 1989), 52.

12.  Otis Baskin and Craig Aronoff, *PUBLIC RELATIONS: The Profession and the Practice*, 2nd ed. (Dubuque, Iowa: Wm. C. Brown Company Publishers, 1988), 178.

13.  "Handling Conflicts: Neutralizing Those Who Resist," *Communications Briefings*, April 1986, 1.

14.  James W. Fowler, *Faith Development and Pastoral Care* (Philadelphia: Fortress Press, 1987), 82-83.

15.  Fowler, *Pastoral Care*, 59.

16.  Ibid., 83.

17.  Elizabeth McMahon Jeep, *The Welcome Table* (Chicago: Liturgical Training Publications, 1982), 4.

18.  James W. Fowler, "Faith Development and Spirituality," *Maturity and the Quest for Spiritual Meaning*, ed. Charles C.L. Kao (Lanham, Maryland: University Press of America, 1988), 21.

19.  Arnold Mitchell, *The Nine American Lifestyles* (New York: Warner Books, 1983), 17.

20.  Ibid., 5-6.

21.  Ibid., 6.

22.  Ibid., 8.

23.  Ibid., 7-8.

24.  Ibid., 9.

25.  Ibid.

26.  Ibid., 89.

27.  Ibid., 10.

28.  Fowler, *Pastoral Care*, 65.

29.  Fowler, "Spirituality," 23.

30.  Ibid., 24.

31.  Fowler, *Pastoral Care*, 88.

32. Mitchell, *Lifestyles*, 10.

33. Murnion, "The Community Called Parish," 10.

34. Ibid., 13.

35. Mitchell, *Lifestyles*, 11.

36. Ibid., 12.

37. Ibid., 98.

38. Ibid., 13.

39. Ibid., 106.

40. Ibid., 15.

41. Ibid., 18.

42. Ibid., 128, 129.

43. Ibid., 19, 20.

44. Ibid., 20-21.

45. Ibid., 21-22.

46. Ibid., 139.

47. Fowler, *Pastoral Care*, 90.

48. Ibid., 91.

49. Ibid., 92.

50. Murnion, "The Community Called Parish," 10.

51. Ibid.

52. Ibid., 11.

53. Ibid., 13.

54. Mitchell, *Lifestyles*, 22.

55. Fowler, "Spirituality," 30.

56. Mitchell, *Lifestyles*, 23.

57. Fowler, *Pastoral Care*, 76.

58. Murnion, "The Community Called Parish," 12.

59. Ibid.

60. Ibid., 14.

61. Fowler, "Spirituality," 30-31.

62. Mitchell, *Lifestyles*, 164.

63. John O'Toole, *The Trouble with Advertising...* (New York: Chelsea House, 1981), 87.

64. David Neff, "Admen for Heaven," *Christianity Today*, September 18, 1987, 13.

65. Ibid.

66. Ibid., 12.

67. Ibid., 13.

68. Kenneth L. Woodward, "From 'Mainline' to Sideline," *Newsweek*, December 22, 1986, 54.

69. Rosalind Silver, "Ad-Ministering: Mighty Messages Make Marketing Memorable," *Media & Values*, Fall 1986, 13.

70. Jay P. Dolan and David C. Leege, "A Profile of American Catholic Parishes and Parishioners: 1820s to the 1980s," *Notre Dame Study of Catholic Parish Life*, 2 (Notre Dame, Indiana: University of Notre Dame, 1985), 6.

71. Aimee L. Stern, "Putting Faith in Madison Avenue," *The New York Times*, December 27, 1987, sec. F, p. 4.

72. Silver, *Media & Values*, 14.

# Chapter 4

# Designing and Sending Messages: Making Connections

Those wonderful people at McDonald's are not only the world's premier purveyors of the fast-food-burger-fries-Coke entrée, but they are also masters of message making and sending.

McDonald's marketing and advertising success lies not just in the words, music and pictures of their messages but in the *planning* and *research* done before a word is committed to paper or a frame of film is shot or a second of advertising time is purchased. The design of every effective advertising campaign begins with an awareness of the strengths and weaknesses of the product or service: what the product/service will do and will not do, what it does better than a competitor's product/service and, conversely, what a competitor's product/service does better.

As discussed in the previous chapter, the effective advertiser also determines exactly who the potential or most likely buyers are for the product and what attitudes, beliefs and perceptions those potential purchasers have of the product. Considerable time and money are then spent in researching what words, music and pictures will be most attractive to those likely buyers. Only then does the work begin on creating and transmitting of the message.

The same is true in any communication: the design and transmission come *last* in the process.[1] Understanding the strengths and weaknesses of the communicator's organization, product, service or role and knowing the audience the communicator wishes to reach are the foundation for creating an effective message. It cannot be over-emphasized: Every message is filtered through the attitudes, experiences, beliefs and values in the listeners' individual and collective psyche—their *frames of reference*. Chapter 3 focused on some of the group attitudes and values present in any parish community.

Regardless of the intended audience, if a message is to have any effect on its target audience, the message must be

- *credible:* People tend to read, watch or listen to messages that present points of view with which they sympathize or in which they have a personal stake. Audiences buy ideas mainly from communicators they trust. And since they often can't test the trustworthiness of the sources themselves, audiences often rely on "trustees" who endorse ideas for them.[2]

- *comprehendible:* The message must be transmitted in a code (words, symbols, images) that the audience is able to "decode." Among the important considerations here are an audience's age and level of education and experience.

- *salient:* The message must be noticed by the audience—it must be sent through a channel that the audience is "tuned" to or connected with (and keep in mind that people tend to expose themselves to communications consistent with their own attitudes).

- *pertinent:* The message must be related to a decision the audience makes when evaluating alternatives (remember: to say "no" or to ignore a message altogether *are* alternatives).

## Elements of an Effective Message

Consider, for a moment, the most effective advertisement you have either read, seen or heard—effective in that the ad "worked" in getting you to buy a product or service or to support a candidate or position. The effectiveness of that ad was the result of four key elements included in the design of that message:

1. *The message (ad) got your attention:* First, the ad was located where you would find it—it might have been in your favorite magazine or on your favorite television program. Secondly, the ad included a funny headline, a catchy slogan or jingle, a beautiful photograph, haunting music or a dramatic exchange that captured your attention. The message *made* you take it in (and remember: the

sponsor spent a great deal of time and money to research exactly what kinds of images you find attractive).

In other words, the ad got and held your attention. That's quite an accomplishment in this era of the "60-second" attention span. All of us are bombarded every day with thousands and thousands of messages, all competing for our attention. Television especially has conditioned viewers to absorb information in 30- and 60-second audio/visual clips. The shrinking human attention span is a major consideration in all message planning and design.

2. *The message illustrated a problem or need you identified with:* The message succeeded in presenting a problem in your life or appealed to a need you seek to fulfill. We all have certain basic needs that we seek to meet in our lives. Among them:

• *physiological needs:* the need for healthy and nutritious food, medical care, clean air, rest.

• *security:* the need for safety and protection.

• *love:* the need for a sense of belonging to family and community (patriotism, for example).

• *self-fulfillment:* the need to feel accomplishment, to make one's dreams for success a reality.

• *esteem:* the need for prestige, status, a sense of accomplishment or competence.

• *meaning in one's life:* the need to be part of something greater than one's own self and to respond to that "otherness."

While individuals seek to fulfill their own needs at different levels of intensity, all individuals experience these basic human needs to some degree in their lives. The most persuasive communicators are those who take the time to discover which specific needs are most dominant in their intended audience and to determine the intensity of emotions in their audience.[3]

3. *The message illustrated how to solve that problem or meet that need.* The message showed you how using the product or service in question would make your life so much better, or how the candidate or position in question would make your nation and/or the world a much better place. The message illustrated the ad-

vantages of the sponsor's approach to the problem or need, or warned of the evils that will befall you if you do not follow the sponsor's approach.

4. *The message showed you how to respond or to act.* Remember that the purpose of any communication is to have an audience *do something* at a specific time and place. This ad motivated you to act: to buy what was being sold, to vote for the candidate being heralded, to support a stand on the issue in question. If the message wanted you to buy, the message might have listed where the product might be purchased or gave a telephone number to call to order the product; if the message sought your participation in a program or event, the message might have included information on where to buy tickets or how to register, as well as when and where the event would take place.

Consider how these elements work in the following two print ads:

# Northwest Airlines: "There's always someone waiting for you at home."

1. *Getting attention:* Monday-through-Friday business travelers are Northwest's target audience here, so the ad was placed in magazines that are read by the kind of upscale, educated and informed people who travel a great deal (this particular ad was taken from *Newsweek* Magazine).

The "attention-getter" here is the wonderful photograph of the baby's face, which runs over two-thirds of the page.

2. *The problem/need presented*: As noted, this ad is targeted to business travelers, but specifically business travelers *with young families*. The ad's headline, "There's always someone waiting for you at home" connects immediately with today's young businessman—and business*woman*!

3. *Solving the problem/meeting the need:* The ad "connects" the business traveler's desire to be home with his/her loved ones with Northwest's "striving to get you there and back, right on schedule"

There's always someone waiting
for you at home.

We know coming home is every bit as important as making your business connections. That's why we're striving to get you there and back, right on schedule. In everything we do, we're working toward new standards of efficiency and comfort. So if you haven't flown with us lately, you should. We're putting the fun back in flying, and the joy in coming back home. For reservations, call your travel agent or Northwest at 1-800-225-2525.

**NORTHWEST AIRLINES**

**Fig. 9.** "There's always someone waiting for you at home." Northwest Airlines.

and the airline's "new standards of efficiency and comfort." The ad creates in the reader's mind a powerful association between Northwest and "the joy of coming home" (the advertising profession calls this concept of associating a product with a consumer's need or want *positioning the product*). "Finally," the tired, battered, stranded, confused and abused air traveler concludes, "here's an airline that understands me and my need to be home with people I love."

4. *The response sought:* Obviously, Northwest wants passengers to make reservations to fly with them, which, the ad points out, is very easy to do with their convenient toll-free 800-number.

- Boston University: *"This door is open for you."*

1. *Getting attention:* Two factors make this ad noticeable to its intended audience. One is its unique size: one third of a standard 8 1/2 x 11" page, but running vertically along the outside column of a page; in a magazine filled with "square boxes" of advertisements, this ad stands out. Secondly, the ad appears in a slick, sophisticated, brash-and-sassy city magazine designed to appeal to young, professional, upscale, urban readership (as well as to those who aspire to be sophisticated, professional and upscale).

The ad's presence in this kind of magazine signals that going back to school is a sophisticated, professional, upscale thing to do.

2. *The problem/need presented*: Note the two lines that are printed in bold type in the ad's text: "The door of opportunity" and "the door to excellence." These "doors" to personal enrichment and career enhancement are very important to this readership.

3. *Solving the problem/meeting the need:* Those wonderful "doors" are opened through Boston University's 500 credit and noncredit courses taught "by instructors who are experts in their fields and committed to their students."

4. *The response sought:* A free schedule of classes and information is available simply by placing a phone call or returning the coupon. In addition, thanks to the university's evening schedule, three locations (accessible by mass transit) and free counseling assis-

## This door is open for you!

**The door to opportunity:** At Metropolitan College, you can earn an undergraduate or graduate degree, take courses for personal enrichment and career enhancement, or enroll in our professional certificate programs.

**The door to excellence:** Study with instructors who are experts in their fields and committed to their students. Choose from more than 500 credit and noncredit courses.

Classes are conveniently scheduled for busy people—in the evenings—at three locations: Boston (on the Green Line), Acton, and Tyngsboro, Massachusetts. Free program-planning assistance is offered to all students by the College's staff of professional academic counselors. Call for your free copy of the current class schedule or mail the coupon below.

**Boston University**
**Metropolitan College**
755 Commonwealth Ave., Boston, MA 02215

**Call 617/353-6000 today!**
Early registration begins Oct. 30, 1989

Please send me a MET College class schedule today.

NAME

ADDRESS

CITY

STATE                    ZIP

TELEPHONE

*An equal opportunity, affirmative action institution*

Fig. 10.
"This door is open for you."
Boston University.

tance and program planning, entering those "doors of opportunity and excellence" is very easy to do.

Most messages that pastors "send" to their congregations can and should work the same way. The key is to show the audience that what you want them to do is in their best interests, that the programs in which you would like them to participate will make their lives more fulfilling, that the donations you would like them to make will support works that embrace their concerns. (Some well-executed examples of these concepts are the creations of the Episcopal Ad Project, discussed in Workshop 3).

# Communications Planning:
# Objectives/Targets/Message/Channels

Every parish and organization does it at one time or another: A group of parishioners work for months to organize, assemble and coordinate a parish program or event. All the necessary arrangements have been made. Every detail has been carefully worked out. But the communications needs of the event are given little thought until the very end. A "public relations committee" is formed with the vague mandate to "let people know about it."

Planning communications should be at the "front end" of every parish event and program. Understanding the dynamics of the communications process and the elements of effective messages should help you construct such a plan.

For a communications program to be effective, it must be based on sound objectives, directed at the right audience, and presented in a fashion that appeals to that audience.[4] The high-powered presentations made by the world's largest advertising and public relations firms to the boards of Fortune 500 corporations are centered around these three factors of *client objectives, target audience* and *key message*.

A parish can develop its own communications plan by considering four questions. The more detailed and specific you are in your answers, the greater chance your communications program will have for success.

1. *What are the objectives of this program?* What is this program or event designed to do? What do you hope to accomplish in this undertaking? How will its success be determined?

Be simple and blunt here. If the bottom line of the program is to raise money, how much? If the objective is to recruit volunteers for a painting project, how many volunteers? If it's to get kids involved in a youth group, what age group? If it's to sell tickets to a parish dinner/dance, how many tickets?

Tip: Think of the objectives here as *verbs*—each objective should begin with the infinitive *to: to* raise money for a new school, *to* sell 300 tickets to the fair, *to* have parents-to-be participate in a baptismal catechesis program.

2. *Who is the principal audience for this program?* Who are you trying to reach with this program? Who do you see as your primary contributors? Who are the principal "consumers" of the program or service you are offering?

Again, specificity is the key here. "Parishioners" is too vague. Which parishioners—parents of young children, senior citizens, those with incomes in the six-figure range? "Youth" is also too large a universe. Do you want to junior high students or high school seniors to participate? Parochial or public school students? Children from single-parent families? Hispanic children?

If the program is for adults, which adults—newly-married, senior citizens, singles, parents? The more specific you are in defining your target audience, the better your chances of reaching them.

List the audiences that need to receive your message, the extent of their interest in the message, what they know about your topic, and what you want them to know about it.

3. *What message do we want to communicate to them?* What do you want to communicate to this audience? What do you want them to know about this program that is most crucial in obtaining their support? *What do you want this audience to do?*

The major consideration here is an analysis of the audience's needs, wants and attitudes. As already discussed, every audience possesses a matrix of opinions and attitudes, based on each person's own personal and unique experiences and his/her identity with a number of different groups. Can a message be developed that identifies the program with the audience's need(s) and shows how the program will meet that need(s)?

**4. *What channels will best communicate this message?*** How do you reach this target audience? What channels and vehicles exist for communicating this message to them? What is the most effective way to tell them about this program or event? *Who* are the most influential opinion leaders with this audience?

Keep in mind in your planning that the more personal and direct your communication with the intended audience, the greater your chances of success. A one-on-one meeting, a phone call or personal letter will secure a "target's" participation or support before the most expensive and glitziest brochure, so concentrate on the personal vehicles first.

Then consider vehicles which will reinforce the message. That's where the brochures, slide-shows, television and radio spots, etc. come into play. Such "mass media" messages must be consistent with the original message articulated above. Communication research has also shown that repetition is a key to reinforcing a message's effectiveness[5]—the more times your audience can see and hear your message, the greater chance your message will "connect."

## Developing a Communications Plan

In addition to the above specifics, an effective communications plan is built on the following foundations:

• *A clear understanding of how this project/event ties into the common mission of the parish.* The youth group's car wash, the community affairs committee's collection of old clothes for the poor, the Holy Name Society's annual trip to the ballpark, the finance committee's study for a new parish catechetical center—how are all of these events and projects part of the common ministry of the parish? Often the connection is obvious; but sometimes it's not so clear. Various members of the parish may very well wonder what this has to do with "church?" If you have planned your communications well, you should be able to answer that.

• *An organizing idea.* A good plan articulates an organizing idea —a central message or theme that is used in all communications: posters, news releases, flyers, pulpit and bulletin announcements, etc. It may be something as simple as the parish going all out to collect food and clothing for a local family in the parish burned out of their home; or it may be a theme that will be used for an extended period of time: "Be part of the life of the parish by volunteering for one of our parish's committees." This organizing idea is then carried through in a slogan, title or graphic symbol used in all communications.

In appealing to Catholics around the country to support the Retirement Fund for Religious, the campaign organizers developed their communications strategy around a single idea: that many of today's most successful professionals were first taught by women religious who dedicated their lives to their students' education. "The price of all that love, it turns out, is $3 billion."

Each year, Merrimack College, located 20 miles north of Boston, sponsors a series of four classical music concerts, featuring artists of national and international renown. The college developed its communication campaign around the idea of "big city concerts without the big city hassles or prices."

In each case, the organizing idea was carried through in every message, from advertisements to news releases.

*A set of specific goals, priorities and deadlines.* Once the brainstorming has been done and all kinds of genuinely superb ideas have been put on the table, hard choices have to be made. It would be great if every idea could be followed through, but workers, time and resources are usually limited. So consider your organization's strengths and weaknesses, as well as the project/event's purposes and goals—and, once again, *specificity* is key—and plan accordingly.

*Some system or mechanism for evaluating the communication program's effectiveness.* As you begin to put the various elements of your communications plan into place, build in ways of tracking responses. If, for example, you use coupons or return cards in

# Communications PLANNING

EVENT/PROJECT:

1. **OBJECTIVE:** *What we seek to accopmplish*

   TO _____

2. **PRINCIPAL AUDIENCE:**
   - Demographic profile:
   - Why this message is important to them:
   - What they know about this program/event/message:
   - Relationship to objective:
   - Opinion leaders/influentials:

3. **SECONDARY AUDIENCE(S):**

4. **MESSAGE:**

5. **ORGANIZING IDEA:**

6. **CHANNELS:**
   - Best approach:
   - Secondary approach(es):
   - Media approaches:  *Radio   Television   Newspapers   Magazines*
     *Parish media: bulletins, newsletters, etc.*
     *Personal contacts*
     *Other*

7. **EVALUATION:** *Tracking responses*

**Fig. 11.** Communications Planning.

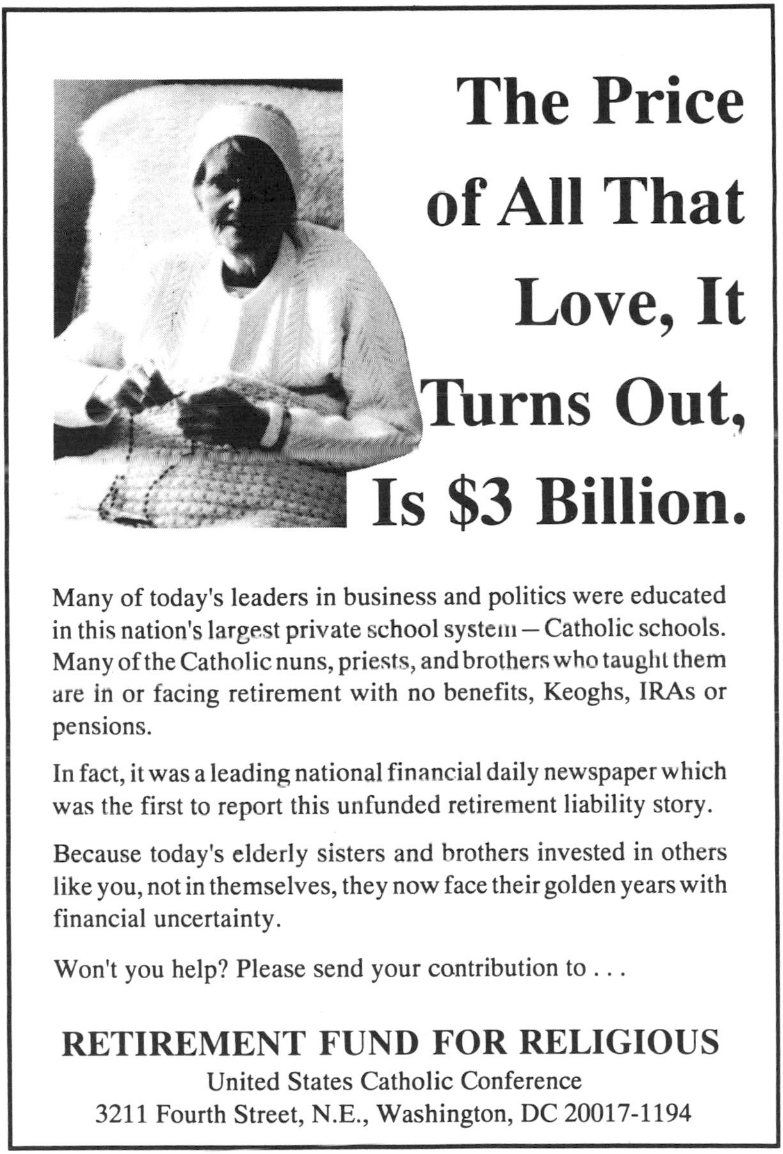

# The Price of All That Love, It Turns Out, Is $3 Billion.

Many of today's leaders in business and politics were educated in this nation's largest private school system — Catholic schools. Many of the Catholic nuns, priests, and brothers who taught them are in or facing retirement with no benefits, Keoghs, IRAs or pensions.

In fact, it was a leading national financial daily newspaper which was the first to report this unfunded retirement liability story.

Because today's elderly sisters and brothers invested in others like you, not in themselves, they now face their golden years with financial uncertainty.

Won't you help? Please send your contribution to . . .

## RETIREMENT FUND FOR RELIGIOUS
United States Catholic Conference
3211 Fourth Street, N.E., Washington, DC 20017-1194

**Fig. 12.** Advertisement for the Retirement Fund for Religious, United States Catholic Conference.

## The 1985-86 Merrimack College Concert Series

All concerts take place in
**The Collegiate Church of Christ the Teacher**
on the Merrimack College campus in North
Andover, Mass.

*Merrimack College is located in North
Andover, Mass., at the junction of Routes
114 and 125, just off either I-93 or I-495.*

Sunday, October 20, 1985
7:30 P.M.
Rosalind Elias
in a concert version of
Bizet's "Carmen"
The Merrimack Valley's own Rosalind Elias
sings the title role in this complete concert
version of Bizet's opera. Appearing with
the Metropolitan Opera star will be Noel Velasco, Robert
Honeysucker, Jane West, Ray Karns, David Stoneman, Andrea
Bradford, Roberta Gilbert, William Cashman, Fred Frabotta and the
Mastersingers of Worcester. F. John Adams will conduct the
Pythagorean Orchestra.

Saturday, March 1, 1986
8 P.M.
The Windsor String Quartet
One of the country's acclaimed
string quartets presents a
program of works by Haydn,
Mendelssohn and Dvorak.

Sunday, December 15, 1985
3 P.M.
Amahl & the Night Visitors
A fully-staged version of Gian Carlo Menotti's
Christmas classic, directed by Albert Brenner
with musical direction by Benjamin Cogen. The
program will also include Corelli's Christmas
Concerto. A Christmas celebration for every
member of the family!

Friday, May 2, 1986, 8 P.M.
The Indian Hill Chamber Orchestra
with guest soloist
Malcolm Lowe, violinist
...ly-appointed concertmaster of the
...a will perform Brahms'
...nder the direction
— Sibelius'

For fur

Merrin
North
(617) 6

# For just about what it costs you to park your car in Boston to attend a concert of the world's finest music, Merrimack College in North Andover will give you the **concert**.

**Fig. 13.** Brochure for the Merrimack College Concert Series, Merrimack College, North Andover, Massachusetts.

various publications, code each ad coupon differently so you'll know how each publication is "pulling" responses for you. In some magazine and newspaper advertisements, for example, you will notice that the return address includes the designation "Department A" or "Department 5C." That "department" is not the section of the company's building that will handle your order. That "department" is a code number given to one of the publications running the ad. If the company receives thousands of coupons addressed to "Department A," then the advertiser knows that the publication which was given the "Department A" designation was an effective advertising "buy" for them. But if the publication which was given the designation "Department B" pulls in a small handful of responses, the company might do well to reconsider advertising there again.

After the project or event is over, evaluate the communications plan for that event. Can you trace ticket sales to specific ads or messages placed? What elements proved to be the most effective in reaching the intended audiences and getting the message to them? Were there any obvious channels of communications that were overlooked?

# Effective Church Communications Planning: Case Studies

The three case studies below illustrate how the elements of communications planning are developed and come together to make a parish project or event work:

## • Case 1: *The Annual Diocesan Appeal*

Each year the Diocese of N. sponsors an annual appeal in all its 135 parishes on behalf of the social and spiritual services sponsored by the diocese. This particular year, the diocese obtained professional communications help, and the following plan was developed.

• *Objectives:* Obviously, the prime objective was (1) to raise money. But the diocese also wanted (2) to create a positive attitude among Catholics for these programs so that they will consider making special gifts and long-term pledges to the appeal, such as deferred giving through bequests.

• *Target audiences:* The Catholics of the area—almost one-third of the state's population—were the prime target. But another key audience was also identified. Appeal organizers realized that the principal opinion leaders and "trustees" in a drive like this are the pastors of the diocese's parishes. Father is the best "salesman" the appeal can have: If Father was enthusiastic about this effort, he would lead his parishioners to support it. A special effort was made, therefore, to solicit the interest and support of pastors.

• *Organizing idea / Messages:* There were two main messages that organizers sought to get across: (1) that many people—*your* neighbors—benefit from the programs and services of the diocese: school children, young couples, the elderly, the homeless, the troubled and the sick; and (2) support for the appeal is one way we meet our responsibility as Catholics to serve one another as Christ served us (a verse from the Gospel reading for Appeal Sunday became the theme for the entire appeal).

• *Channels:* The pastors became a key channel for the campaign. Every pastor in the diocese was invited to one of several luncheon meetings held throughout the diocese exclusively for them. Approaching the pastors as co-workers in the appeal, the diocese showed them exactly how *their* parishes benefited from these programs. Support materials, such as homily outlines and bulletin inserts, were designed to help them "present" the appeal to their parishioners (special care was also taken not to overwhelm them with reams of useless promotionals, but to supply pastors only with materials they wanted and could use).

Newspaper stories as well as television spots, posters and brochures emphasized stories of "your neighbors" served by diocesan services. Distributed with the appeal envelope was a card listing all diocesan services and agency telephone numbers, inviting all Catholics to make use of these services.

• *Evaluation:* The donations, obviously, are the prime indicator of the campaign's effectiveness; but also important in gauging the success of this communications effort is discovering *which* parishes were the most generous to the appeal, the extent of that pastor's involvement in the campaign and what messages he used to interest his parishioners in the appeal.

- **Case 2:** *The Cathedral Lunchtime Concert Series*

    The diocesan cathedral is located in the middle of the downtown business district. There is a small plaza in the front, with benches. During the early spring (right after Easter) the social committee organized a series of noontime outdoor concerts, featuring local musicians from area colleges and conservatories.

    - *Objectives:* (1) To invite shoppers and workers on their lunch breaks to spend a beautiful spring lunch hour enjoying music in the cathedral plaza; (2) to provide an opportunity for local artists to perform; (3) to identify the cathedral with the life of the city,

    - *Target audiences:* Workers (secretaries, clerks, etc.) in the downtown district, shoppers, the parish and community at-large. Major "opinion leaders": the local chamber of commerce, the local daily newspaper and radio station.

    - *Organizing idea / Messages:* Come, celebrate a new spring in Cathedral Plaza—Bring your lunch and enjoy music beautifully performed by area musicians.

    - *Channels:* Invitations to the series were sent to all of the offices and companies within walking distance of the cathedral (the most personal and effective approach the committee could take). Posters were placed in all area stores. The local newspaper and radio station were informed of the concert schedule, resulting in a series on each of the performers and in a newspaper series of free promotional spots and interviews with the performers on the local classical radio station. Many of the artists who performed in the series also had "channels" of communications with their own audiences which the series planners were able to utilize, such as the college communities where the members of one of the string groups taught music.

    - *Evaluation:* Again, numbers are the obvious success gauge; but an important question here is *where* the numbers of attendees come from, *how* they learned of the program, *what* attracted them to the program (the musical selections? the performers? the time of day?). One method of obtaining this important information is to include a reply card in the program. In order to encourage them to fill the card out and return it, invite the audience to become part of the producing organization's mailing list for news of future concerts and programs. Along with space for their names and addresses, include a question or two inquiring as to how they heard about this series.

## • Case 3: *Lenten Vespers*

The parish liturgist and music director planned the celebration of Evening Prayer ("Lenten Vespers") on Wednesday evenings at 7 P.M. during the season of Lent. The minister at a local Protestant church, with a reputation as an excellent preacher, was invited to preach at each service.

*Objectives:* To invite as many parishioners as possible to share in the service of Evening Prayer, the prayer of the Church.

*Target audiences:* The adults of the parish especially, but anyone in the community would be welcomed (especially members of the guest preacher's parish).

*Organizing idea / Messages:* This Wednesday night series is a way of doing something special to "keep Lent" as a time for individual renewal and re-creation. "Vespers" is an attempt to bring back a traditional but no less meaningful form of community prayer (an appeal directed especially to those "traditionalists" who remember Wednesday evening Lenten "devotions"). An opportunity to hear a preacher acknowledged as one of the best and most creative in our area (a concept appealing to those who value contemporary ecumenical approaches to spirituality).

*Channels:* Parish publications, especially the bulletin, included information on the series several weeks before the beginning of Lent. Various bulletin announcements explained the format and history of Evening Prayer, introduced the guest preacher, and explained the meaning of the different elements of the ritual (the use of light and incense, for example). Neighboring parishes were invited to attend through letters to their pastors asking that a notice be placed in their bulletins. Local newspapers, informed of the series, published stories on the ecumenical dimensions of the Vesper series.

- *Evaluation:* Attendance *may* be the major criterion for judging the success of a series like this—but perhaps success is determined not in quantity of participation, but in *quality* of participation. What did this experience mean to the participants? Was it the occasion of prayer and renewal that the planners had hoped? Only the participants can share that, so planners of such events should make it a point to talk informally to participants after the services, perhaps even calling some who become "regulars" each week and ask them what these services meant to them, what impelled them to participate each week and if they would participate in similar services again.

As you read the above sketches of what other parishes and dioceses planned in those situations, you may very well have thought of other possibilities and opportunities. The idea is that designing and sending messages effectively are the result of planning and research.

Effective message sending begins with a realistic and sober assessment—warts and all—of your organization, product, service, position or candidate, and a clear understanding of your intended audience's beliefs, attitudes and perceptions of your organization, organizations like yours, and you, the communicator. From that collected data, a message is designed. As well as getting the target audience's attention, the most effective messages are those that present or position the communicator's intended response in the context of fulfilling a need or solving a problem the audience is experiencing.

Message-sending is not an isolated, scatter-shot process. It is a process that requires planning and the organization of objectives, target audiences and key messages. But even the best plan is just a piece of paper until it is put into action. How to put your communications plan into action through the use of the various media available to your parish is the focus of the next two chapters.

## *WORKSHOP*: Writing for the Media

Writing news is a special skill, but a skill that just about anyone can master if he/she

- understands what and why an event is news and
- can write a complete sentence.

The standard news release is still a major conduit of information between organizations like your parish and the news media. Today, news releases are written primarily to convince one person—the editor or the news director—that its content is news that it should be published or broadcasted.

It may sound like a cliché, but the six points essential to a good news release/story still are the "5 Ws and H"—Who, What, Where, When, Why and How. In every story, one of those Ws (or the H) is that most important element that makes this story news. That element should be displayed in the very first sentence and paragraph of your story—what is called, in the news business, the *lead* or *hook*. A good lead tells immediately why this story is important in order to arouse the reader's curiosity and a desire for more information.

If you have a good news sense, you can recognize immediately which of the five Ws/H is the lead and frame the lead sentence accordingly. Consider the following leads:

Lead: *WHO?*   The *new Archbishop of Boston* will pay his first visit to the Lowell area on Sept. 28.

Lead: *WHAT?*   A coalition of five local churches have established *the city's first food pantry* for the poor and families in crisis.

Lead: *WHERE?*   A Maryknoll missionary will present her eye witness account of life in *the guerrilla-controlled zones of El Salvador* in a special lecture at St. Luke's Parish.

Lead: *WHEN?*   The *Christmas season* begins at Our Lady of Peace Parish on Sunday, Dec. 3, when the Parish Chorale presents an Advent concert of chants and Christmas folk songs from around the world.

Lead: *HOW?*    The 200 families of St. Margaret's Parish have committed themselves *to skipping dinner on the Wednesdays of Lent for the hungry of Africa.*

As you can see, often one or more of the Ws/H can be part of the lead. The trick, however, is to play up *the* element of the story that makes this news. One way to help you determine the lead is to pretend you are about to run into the next room and tell someone this "news." What would be the first fact out of your mouth? In all probability, that first thing would be the lead.

The lead sentence should be a paragraph by itself. The next paragraph should include the remaining four Ws/H.

The third and following paragraphs should go into the details of your story. Each succeeding paragraph should be of *declining* importance. Professionals call this writing technique the *inverted pyramid.* It permits the editor/news director to pick up the important facts of your story in the first few lines. Then, if he/she does not have space or time to use the whole release, the story can be cut from the bottom, where the least important details are given.

As you write a news story:

* Keep the writing style simple. Keep away from superlatives and superfluous language. Never use a word in a news release that you would not use in everyday conversation. Keep the language simple, direct and to the point.

* Be brief! Almost every news story can be written on one double-spaced typewritten page—two pages maximum.

* Write short sentences and short paragraphs. Two sentences usually make a good paragraph in a news release.

* The city editor of a metropolitan daily says that, whether writing a lead for a story or calling an editor with an idea, you have about 10 seconds to capture the editor's attention. Be persistent, but remember that most editors lose interest after 10 seconds—remember: yours is not the only news release the editor/producer will be receiving that day. Also avoid leads that begin, "The Rev. N. announced today . . ." What happened is more important than who said it or made it happen.

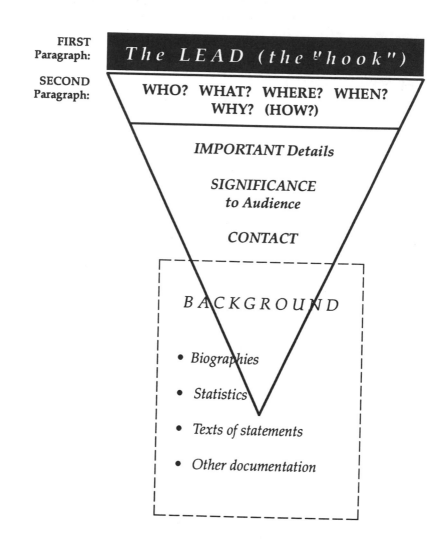

**Fig. 14.** The "inverted pyramid" technique of newswriting.

- Don't editorialize or give opinions in a news release, unless it is a quote from someone involved in the story and the quote amplifies the news.

- Check and double-check facts, figures, grammar and spelling. Never guess on dates, times, places or names.

- A number of professional writing style books are available from local book stores. These manuals answer such "style" questions as what should be abbreviated and how, rules on punctuation, and the use of titles. Perhaps the best (and available in paperback editions in most bookstores) is *The New York Times Manual of Style and Usage.*

- Always include the name, address and telephone number of the contact person the news editor/director can call for more information—and be ready to help them with more information, arrangements for interviews with principals—whatever they need to cover the story—*your* story.

- Most news releases, if they are well-written and present a good, newsworthy lead, will be considered by *both* the *print* and *electronic* (radio and television) media.

- Target releases to *specific* media with *specific* audiences— the days of what was called "papering the media" with the same generic, multipage release are over. Don't get the reputation for sending "junk" releases. After a while, an envelope with your name and address on it will not even be opened before it is thrown away.

- Many editors of smaller publications (especially weeklies and small dailies) appreciate good photography that accompany stories. They also place a premium on good writing because they have smaller staffs to edit and rewrite material.

- If you have both a FAX machine and a good story, FAX your story to the media. A sample news release in the standard format appears on the next page.

---

Blessed Sacrament Parish          Contact:    John Tucker
111 Leandre Drive                             Jeanne St. Onge
Hometown, USA 99999                           Parish Social Concerns
Telephone: (000) 555-5555                     Committee

FOR IMMEDIATE RELEASE                         Date prepared: January 24, 199_

Advisory:  PRACTICAL SOLUTIONS, BASIC INFORMATION FOCUS OF
           FEBRUARY 10 CONFERENCE ON ENVIRONMENTAL ISSUES
           AT BLESSED SACRAMENT PARISH


What individuals, families and parish communities can do to protect the environment will be the focus of a conference on Saturday, February 10, at Blessed Sacrament Parish.

"Faithful Stewards of Creation," sponsored by the Blessed Sacrament Social Concerns Committee, will begin at 9:30 A.M. and conclude at 3:00 P.M. in the Parish Catechetical Center at 113 Leandre Drive. All interested persons are invited to participate.

John Tucker, conference chairman, explained that "our goal is to make people aware of the seriousness of the environmental crisis but also to give them a sense that there are steps everyone can take that will make a difference."

Guest speakers at the conference will include Dr. Paul Turmel, assistant professor of ecology at the University of Massachusetts; Leonard Parker of the Hometown engineering department; and Kelly Jamieson, a free-lance writer on the environment whose articles have appeared in *Smithsonian World*, *New England Nature* Magazine and many other national magazines on science and the environment.

Following each presentation, participants will have the opportunity to ask whatever questions they may have regarding environmental issues.

A registration fee of $5 covers the cost of materials and a light lunch. As space is limited, pre-registration is requested. More information is available from the Blessed Sacrament Social Concerns Committee, 111 Leandre Drive, Hometown, USA 99999 (555-5555).

---

**Fig. 15.** A sample news release. Note the format, including the *advisory*, a one-line summary of the news angle, written to "hook" news directors and editors into the story.

Mary, Queen of Peace Parish
Turnpike Road
East Anytown, USA 99999
Telephone: (000) 555-5555

Contact:   Rev. Robert Smith
Patricia Dinsmore
Parish Youth Ministers

FOR IMMEDIATE RELEASE                Date prepared: February 15, 199_

Advisory: COLLEGE STUDENTS FROM QUEEN OF PEACE TO SPEND
THEIR SPRING BREAK WORKING WITH POOR AND ELDERLY
IN MAINE CO-OP

While many college students spend their spring break on the beaches of
Florida, a group of eight college students from Mary, Queen of Peace Parish
will spend their week off from classes at the opposite, colder end of the At
lantic seacoast.

The eight students have volunteered to spend their March 14-18 break
working in Orland, Maine, with H.O.M.E.—Homeworkers Organized for
More Employment—a cooperative organized for low income families. The
eight students, to be accompanied by Rev. Robert Smith and Patricia
Dinsmore who direct the young adult group at Queen of Peace Parish, will
spend the week insulating the homes of low-income elderly residents, working in the co-op's sawmill and shinglemill, and working in the co-op's nur-
sery and tutoring programs for students from low income families.

"Last Summer, during a weekend retreat the students talked about doing
something different, something constructive during the week they had off."
Father Smith explained. "They asked me to look into some places where
they could spend their week off doing something that will make a difference."

Father Smith contacted the H.O.M.E. through the Catholic Diocese of
Portland, Maine.

Making the trip to Orland will be Frank Bell, a sophomore at the

(MORE)

**Fig. 16.** This news release is more "feature-oriented" rather than
hard (specifically timed) news.

## • *Public Service Announcements*

Many radio and television stations carry some type of community bulletin board announcements. They are usually short, 20-25 words, but contain all the required information (the five Ws and the H). Most stations require that such announcements be sent at least two weeks in advance; smart parish communicators send them it at least *four* weeks in advance.

Some radio stations will consider longer messages of 10, 20 and 30 seconds. Such time is usually given to long-term campaigns and projects requiring considerable planning (a walk for hunger, a social action program, support for an ongoing project like a soup kitchen).

PSAs of this kind should be written much like a community bulletin board announcement. Keep the language simple and conversational. Some stations will invite you to record the message yourself or have one of their announcers record it.

Talk to your local station program director or public service director and ask what their policies are regarding PSAs. Occasionally, a station will become so taken with a local community project that they "adopt it" as a station project. Don't be afraid to ask if the station would sees any promotional possibilities for itself through your project.

The most important rule to keep in mind when sending material to the media is to *always remember the particular audience of the publication/station.* Is this story important to them?

A final thought: The principles of good newswriting are not only useful in sending out news releases and public service copy; many of same techniques can and should also be utilized in just about every form of message-sending—from writing your parish bulletin to composing an advertisement for the local newspaper.

For as little as an hour or two a week, you could make the difference in somebody's life. The Good Samaritan Hospice volunteers provide terminally ill individuals and their families with respite care, transportation, companionship and help with light house work and errands. The time you give could be the high point of the week for someone—and for you, too! To find out more about becoming a hospice volunteer, call Ellen Casserly at Good Samaritan Hospice at 555-5555.

"The New Parent's Survival Kit" is a series of four Thursday night programs for new parents and parents-to-be. The sessions will take place on Thursday evenings, October 3 through October 24 at St. Teresa's Parish at 7:30 P.M. Basic baby care, dealing with the strain of a new baby on a marriage and family financial planning will be among the topics to be discussed by professionals in the child care and family counseling fields. For more information, call St. Teresa's Parish at 555-5555.

**Fig.17.** Sample radio scripts:

TOP: This 30-second Public Service Announcement for an on-going program is written to interest listeners in the joys and sense of fulfillment one can experience from volunteer work.

BOTTOM: The script for a community bulletin board announcement includes just the basic information (the 5Ws and H).

Note how *both* scripts end with a telephone number listeners can call for more information.

# Notes

1. Tony Schwartz, *The Responsive Chord* (Garden City, New York: Anchor Press/Doubleday, 1973), 26.

2. Anthony Fulginiti, "Using the Most Successful Persuasive Techniques," *Communications Briefings*, April 1986, 8a.

3. Harry Hazel, *The Power of Persuasion* (Kansas City, Missouri: Sheed & Ward, 1989), 32.

4. Paula Marantz Cohen, *A Public Relations Primer: Thinking and Writing in Context* (Englewood Cliffs, New Jersey: Prentice-Hall, Inc., 1987), 49.

5. Larry Lauer, "Eight Steps to a PR Plan," *Currents,* January 1986, 30.

# Chapter 5

# Media Relations I: Playing 'Offense'

Football is a game of offense and defense. The team playing offense is in control of the ball, trying to move it downfield into the opponent's territory for a touchdown. When the opposition has the ball, the team then goes on defense, trying to keep its opponent from marching through its territory.

Relations with the mass media—radio, television and the press is a "game" of offense and defense. Sometimes you control the "ball"—you have a message you want to get across to people through the media. Your approach must be more aggressive: you have to "move" the story into the "territory" of the news directors and editors.

Then there are times, as Johnson & Johnson, Exxon and hundreds of once-prominent politicians have painfully experienced, when the media carry the ball, when they want to tell a story and will run right through *your* territory to tell it. If you don't know all the rules of the media game or you have a poorly-prepared game plan, you can be run down in the process.

The next two chapters focus on a parish's relations with the media. This chapter looks at "offense"—when you have a story or message you believe should be covered in the local newspaper or carried on your local radio or television station.

## Defining *News*

Typically, a parish considers the messages it wants to communicate through the media as *news*.

Exactly what is *news*?

It depends, as do all messages in communications, on the audience.

The nature of the audience is the determining factor in what a news organization covers and publishes or airs. The same demographic factors that determine how any message is designed and transmitted also determine what is news. What the president of IBM considers news differs significantly from what a farmer in the nation's heartland considers news; what is of interest and importance to an accountant in Boston may go unnoticed by the college student in California; the issues that concern retirees are not the same as those important to young, working parents.

Two criteria dictate the selection of news items for a publication or program: those stories which are of the greatest *significance* to an audience, and those stories which are of greatest *interest* to an audience.[1] News directors and editors base their news judgments by applying to a potential story a set of *news values*. An event is news if it possesses one or more of the following attributes:

- *impact*: events that are likely to affect many people, especially people in that particular media's coverage or market area;
- *timeliness*: events that are immediate and recent;
- *prominence*: events involving well-known (famous or infamous) persons and institutions;
- *proximity*: people or events in a particular publication's or station's coverage or market area that reflect a national trend or play a significant role in a major national or international event (the "local angle" to a story), or events that have significance beyond the immediate region;
- *conflict*: the stuff of which all great stories are made;
- *newness*: the novel, the different, the just-discovered, the "bizarre";
- *currency*: situations and events that relate to issues under current discussion in public forums.

In presenting a story to the media, then, ask the questions that the editors, producers, writers and reporters will be asking: *Who will consider this news, and how significant and of what interest is this news to them?*

## Market-driven Media

A generation ago, newspapers, radio and television stations sought the largest audience possible—mass media sought the masses. But the explosion in communications technologies has resulted in an information "glut." There are very few "mass media" today; editors and producers, instead, target their publications and programming to attract carefully determined and identifiable readerships and viewerships.

Consider, for example:

• the growth in the number of channels for electronic communication: since the early 1950s, the number of AM radio stations has doubled, FM is up fivefold, television outlets have multiplied, and almost 70 percent of American homes have access to cable television;[2]

• computerized print production, enabling faster and cheaper production of books and specialized magazines;

• the increased output and speed of communications made possible by satellite, computer and fiber optics, which have led to new "national" media: *USA Today*, cable television, direct mail marketing.

In order to survive, most commercial broadcast stations and newspapers do *not* seek *every* listener, *every* viewer and *every* reader in their markets. They seek, instead, to serve a *specific segment* of that total audience with information and programming that particular audience segment wants. With over 100 radio stations coming into as diverse a city as New York, for example, the idea of there being a single "number one" station is meaningless. Stations, therefore, develop their own format for attracting some portion of the total listenership. There are radio stations that specialize in all-news programming, in all-talk programming, and in every possible music style and preference, from classical to country, from big bands to rock.

The decision as to what audience segment to appeal to is made only after considerable study and research. As in any communications process, the same questions about audiences' demographics, attitudes, perceptions, beliefs, needs and interests are studied by publishers and programmers before designing their publications and formats. Broadcasting and publishing, as established in the United States, exist primarily to deliver a specific commodity to paying advertisers. That commodity is *us*—the characteristics, buying power, wants, needs and hopes of each viewer, listener and reader.[3] The essence of good media relations is the ability to find a story that connects with a parish goal that is, at the same time, something that a newspaper or television or radio station wants.[4]

A look at how various forms of media operate today will clarify how this concept of audience selection works and what it means to the parish communicator in terms of planning messages and approaching the media.

### • *Daily newspapers*

Newspapers are the *one* means of reaching a *general* audience in this age of specialized media targeted to segmented audiences. Although no longer the dominant medium, newspapers are still a powerful force in shaping the public agenda and influencing public discussion. Because they reach most of their readers on a daily basis, newspapers are the single most effective medium for a publicity build-up and promotional campaign. Research indicates that daily newspapers are read, generally, by interested, influential people—although the typical daily reader actually reads one-fifth to one-fourth of the news content of the paper.[5]

The current trends in newspaper journalism are a microcosm of what is happening in the media in general: a daily newspaper's total readership consists of many smaller audiences with special interests rather than one mass readership. Dailies, therefore, publish several different sections under the banners of news, regional news, "living," the arts, business and sports. One notable outgrowth of this trend has been the development and improvement of the business and financial sections of daily newspapers, economics being one area that newspapers can cover more effectively than television.

With this trend in special sections has developed the role of the reporter-specialist. Events are not only chronicled but put into some kind of perspective by journalists assigned to such "beats" as science, the arts, education and religion. These "beat" reporters who cover the issues and concerns of the various ministries of the parish are important people for parish communicators to know. Parishes and church groups often have people with expertise who can be valuable sources to these writers. An effective parish communications program includes identifying these resource people and making them known to reporters and available for these kinds of background stories.

The success of *USA Today* and its emergence as a national newspaper has had a major impact on the content and design of all daily newspapers. The publishers of *USA Today* have sought to publish a paper for a readership weaned on television. *USA Today* is primarily responsible for a new style in daily newspapers: shorter stories, more graphs and charts, "factoid" sidebars and a greater use of color. The impact of this trend towards short, clear, factual stories should not be lost on parish communicators who submit stories to their area dailies (the editors of parish bulletins and newsletters should also take careful note of this *USA Today*-style trend).

Most daily newspapers started as evening publications, but television news has claimed the evening news audience. Most of today's dailies (especially the large, metropolitan dailies) have survived in the age of television by publishing in the morning. Keep that in mind when planning stories—be aware of their deadlines.

The largest of all newspaper circulations belongs to the Sunday newspapers. Sunday papers are usually (though not always) edited and produced by special news staffs. Because readers have more time on weekends to spend with a newspaper, Sunday editions place a heavy emphasis on feature articles and columns on special interests and groups (such as stamp collecting, gardening, schools and senior citizens). Sunday newspapers, therefore, offer special opportunities to the parish communicator.

## • *Weekly newspapers*

The majority of weekly newspapers serve communities and regions that cannot draw enough advertising support for a daily publication.  By no means, however, are all weekly newspapers small-town, rural phenomena.  The reality is that many suburban communities, living in the shadows of major cities with large metropolitan dailies, are served by successful—and *read*—weekly publications that report on the local people, events and issues which receive little or no coverage in the large dailies but are no less important to these residents.

On the "high" end of the weekly newspaper spectrum are those weeklies that are written, edited and managed like small daily newspapers; at the "low" end are the free weekly "shoppers," with pages and pages of advertising, with just enough news releases and feature material to fill whatever space in the paper remains unsold to advertisers.  The majority of the America's thousands of weekly newspapers fall somewhere in the middle of this spectrum.

Practically all weekly newspapers are run with very small staffs.  Editors welcome well-written material and usable black-and-white photographs from just about any source—including the local parish.  Another common characteristic of all weeklies is a Tuesday or Wednesday deadline for a Thursday publication day, in order to accommodate advertising geared to the weekend shopper.

## • *Television*

Television is a medium of pictures—without pictures, there is no story.  In approaching television stations, the first question a parish communicator has to ask is: *Is this story VISUAL enough for television?*  What can the local television station come and take pictures—*moving* pictures—of?  In "pitching" a story to a news producer, a parish communicator must lay out a story with a beginning, a middle and an end and enough impact that commuters will talk about it on the next morning's train.  Usually, this must be accomplished within a minute and a half.[6]

Remember that *time* is the premium commodity in television and radio.  Commercial television devotes about 10 percent of its airtime to news and the remaining 90 percent to entertainment; and of that 10 percent, only 20-22 minutes of every 30 minutes is actual news.  A good parish story has to translate visually and quickly to be of interest to a television news operation.

A reporter for a major metropolitan television station offers this explanation of the kinds of stories television news departments cover:

> The most important element of our daily work is breaking news. If [your parish] is involved in a high-impact event of NEWS value, call the assignment desk and give clear, concise details to them. Stress the immediacy of the "breaking news." If you want to lose credibility with assignment desk people (great friends, formidable enemies), try pulling the wool over their eyes about something being "breaking news." It might get you one story; it will also get you permanently out the door.
>
> In the next category of immediacy fall stories which can be seen as "follow-ups" to breaking news: there's a highjacking in Athens and (you run) all airport security firm. We're interested—same day or next day.
>
> Then comes the whole spectrum of stories which we would consider general topic, without a time factor or with a much looser time specificity. News still wants these stories, but we're so tied up with breaking news responsibilities that we sometimes are hard to get through to.
>
> Many stories, even good ones, don't get done because of non-judgmental factors: other stories planned for the same date, availability of cameras, breaking news that forces us to cancel at the last moment. There's no predictability (or fairness) to it, but it's the nature of the business. I call the people in our business "adrenaline vampires"—we feed on the rush of the intensity, the excitement of change and uncertainty . . . We rarely control the raging river—we just ride it.[7]

Local stations find news coverage costly and welcome an assist from the source who can provide them with newsworthy video. A parish increases its chances of making the evening television news if the parish approaches the right person at the station (usually that person is the assignment editor, the individual responsible for assigning reporters and camera crews to cover stories) and if the parish communicator can articulate the news values of the story and the possibilities for pictures.

Advances in television technology mean constant change and new opportunities in television programming and journalism. One example: local television stations are challenging the networks' dominance in covering national and international stories. Local station news departments are always looking for the local angle to national events and trends. Can your church group or parish "plug in" to such coverage with information, events and experts from your parish staff?

## • *Cable access*

Cable television offers the local parish possibilities for its own long-form programming through local access channels—channels reserved by the local cable operator for local groups to produce and air their own programs.

Successful cable programming demands three ingredients that are in short supply in many parishes:

- expertise in the technical side of television;
- dedicated people who understand the potential and limits of television; and
- a carefully formed plan to develop an audience for the program.

  While volunteers can supply the first two items, the parish leadership must supply the third—and it is this third element that sinks many local parish cable television efforts. As much time and resources should be devoted to letting the audience know about the program as are devoted to producing the show itself.

If your parish has the talent and vision for cable television, talk to your local cable operator about the opportunities available to groups like your parish. There are also several excellent resource books and guides available to parish groups who wish to begin a cable television "ministry."

## • *Radio*

Radio is the medium that refuses to die. Radio has, in fact, thrived in the television age because, first, it concentrates on serving as a *local* medium, featuring programming of interest to the local community; and secondly, radio has been most successful in developing special programming formats to attract audiences.

According to the Radio Advertising Bureau, radio remains a very strong source of news for most people in the country, especially in the morning, and for almost half (49 percent) it is the first source of news in the morning (television is second, with 29 percent, and newspapers third, with 15 percent). Radio is the first source of news when any local emergency occurs. Other surveys indicate that 77 percent of the opinion leaders in a community listen to radio news first thing in the morning.[8] The Associated Press Broadcast Services, in a study of 1,000 adults, found that an astonishing 70 percent said they pay as much or more attention to news and information on the radio as they do to the music, and 69 percent said that the main reason they listen to radio is to keep up with the latest news events.[9]

Radio's peak listening times are morning and afternoon "drive" times, so called because most listeners are in their cars. The largest audiences tune in—and the highest advertising rates are charged—during the 6-9 A.M. and 3-7 P.M. "drive times."

Because of the technical dimensions of its cleaner, static-free signal, most FM stations program music formats; AM stations have turned to news, information and talk formats. Hundreds of different radio formats have been tried around the country, including all-sports (which has been successful), all-comedy and even all-Elvis Presley music (which have not), so no list of radio formats will be complete; but among the *major* radio formats that are heard in just about all parts of the country are the following:

- *Adult contemporary*: These stations program popular music (easier, "softer" rock music), news and information, with some talk shows and sports programming (usually in the evening). Appealing to middle-age adult audiences, adult contemporary radio stations place special emphasis on promoting their announcers, disk jockeys and talk show hosts. On these stations, the best opportunities for the parish communicator are in newscasts; in submitting public service announcements, which the station airs free of charge as time permits (but don't expect great play during drive times); and in making knowledgeable and articulate guests available for locally-produced talk shows.

Many of these same communications opportunities offered to parishes on adult contemporary stations are available (news, public service announcements), although usually to a lesser extent, on stations that specialize in different kinds of music formats, geared to specific audiences:

- *Classical music*: Radio stations that broadcast classical music programs have relatively small but very loyal audiences—sophisticated, well-educated and affluent.

- *Country music*: Country radio stations have significant audience shares in every region of the country (even urban areas). The audience is usually older, less educated and not as affluent.

- *Classic hits/soft rock format:* These stations play songs from the 1960s, '70s and '80s in order to appeal to "baby boomers" who grew up listening to this music. The "thirty-something" audience is professional, well-educated and urban-centered.

- *All-news:* Professional, older adults form the primary audience of all-news radio (a very expensive format for stations to maintain). Although they have lower ratings overall than music stations, listeners to all-news stations are *active* listeners—they have a higher retention level of what they hear. All-news stations use a great deal of material. Good, dependable, informative news sources are highly valued by these news directors.

- *All-talk:* This format appeals to adults, mostly middle-age and older. Listeners are not as affluent and are generally less-educated than listeners to all-news stations, but are just as "active" in listening and retaining messages. Parish organizations may have the opportunities to place guests on some of these programs.

Again, these are just some of the basic radio formats that your parishioners are listening to.

*Brevity* and *sound* are the main ingredients in effective radio writing and production. Radio news departments use short, to-the-point news stories written for the *ear*. And stories will receive more airtime if accompanied by brief 30-45 second interview clips (called *actualities*) with newsmakers and sources. As does every good news-gathering and reporting operation, radio news reporters keep an active telephone file of good, dependable, knowledgeable and articulate sources to interview for actualities.

• *Public service time*

Most television and radio stations offer free public service time to nonprofit organizations. Getting public service announcements (PSAs) on television especially is becoming increasingly competitive. Television stations are swamped with requests from charitable organizations to air their messages. The most effective way to obtain PSA time is to talk with the station's public service director, that person who controls every public service announcement that goes on the air on a given telvision station.

Because it is more locally-oriented than its visual cousin, radio public service directors are much more open to local organizations as well as to services and agencies that relate to their audiences.

• **Talk and interview programs**

Talk and interview programs are a staple of radio and television programming. Formats include the magazine programs (*60 Minutes*), the *Donahue* and *Oprah*-style interview shows, the news and information programs with a different guest and topic for each seven-minute segment (*The Today Show*), and radio talk shows, most of which invite listeners to call in questions. In this age of specialized media, there are many talk programs on both television (especially cable) and radio that focus on one area or topic: from money management to auto repair.

In *The Talk Show Book,* Pat McMillen, producer of *Donahue,* says the best way to approach a talk or interview program with a guest and topic idea is by letter:

> I like to see only one or two pages about the show idea. Because our show has a fairly singular focus, I want their idea stated very succinctly. For example, if their idea is a diet they have developed for dealing with hyperactive children, that's all the first line has to say. "I have an idea for how you can stop hyperactivity in children through the use of a specialized diet." In the next paragraph, they may outline the diet in brief, perhaps listing five or ten main points. They should explain the reason this diet works. The next paragraph should tell how and why the writer became interested in this issue. He should list his credentials, never lying about or embellishing them. If he's appeared on other programs, that could be included within the credentials section. The last paragraph should give day and night phone numbers, asking that the producer call if interested. Finally, he should include the article or the book [he's written], if there is one. Production offices need only one copy of these materials, not four or five, as are sometimes sent. I prefer that manuscripts not be sent. People writing to shows should never send their only copy of manuscripts or anything else.
>
> It is possible that these items can be lost in the volume of mail.[10] Whatever material you send to a talk program producer, the entire "package" should take no more than 15 minutes to read.[11] As well as your cover letter and the items mentioned above, another item to send, if possible, are newspaper clippings about your guest or topic.[12]

## • *Magazines, Newsletters and Other Publications*

Most magazines and newsletters today are targeted to specific audiences—special interest groups who value certain kinds of information because of their occupations, social affiliations and interests. There is a magazine or periodical catering to almost every known interest, business, industry, vocation and hobby in America. There are magazines and newsletters today for Boy Scouts, religious educators, tennis players and garbage collectors.

With the exception of *LIFE* Magazine and the news weeklies, the days of the general circulation magazine are over. These are the golden days of the city and regional magazines. These publications are targeted to a specific city or region of the country. Editorially, they appeal to the "right" advertising demographics—young, upscale, sophisticated, college-educated, urban dwellers. Their pages include a mix of service articles (health and fitness, beauty, travel, finance, restaurant guides), humor and "glamor" (media and personalities), and listings of local entertainment events and the arts.

If your parish has an idea for a story that you think is of interest to a specific magazine, approach the editor with it (usually through a complete but concise letter). Be prepared to articulate clearly why this story would be of interest to the publication's readers. If the idea is accepted, be prepared to work with the magazine's staff or a freelance writer assigned to the story.

Major organizations and institutions today often have their own "in house" magazines and newsletters. Who are the major employers in your parish? What service organizations do your parishioners belong to? Is a college or university located within your parish? Institutions and organizations like these all have employee and membership publications of some kind. Would they accept ideas and news releases from your parish—and can you make your case to them why their audiences would be interested in what your parish is all about?

• *Advertising*

If you seek to retain total control of your message, paid advertising is the best way to proceed. "Paid," however, is the operative word here. By buying the time or space for your message, you control the content, approach, style, treatment and, to a great extent, the audience for your message. If your budget permits the purchase of advertising (and most parish program budgets, with more insightful and careful planning, could), consider both your *message* and the *medium*.

*Television* is very expensive and demands a great deal of advanced planning and work to be effective. Not only does the advertiser pay for the air time but also for the production of the commercial itself, which can be very expensive depending on a number of factors: location shooting, the visual effects used, actors and talent needed. If your project and budget warrant a television campaign, contact the sales department of your local television station.

*Radio* advertising is considerably less expensive. Compared to television, radio commercials can be produced quickly and inexpensively. The cost of the ad varies according to its length (60 seconds and 30 seconds are standard in radio) and the time of day it airs: morning and afternoon drive times are most expensive, followed by mid-day; evening and late-night times are considerably less expensive.

Radio sales departments are happy to talk with prospective advertisers. They can help you develop a schedule of ads that fits your budget, as well as help in writing and producing the ad itself. Some stations even have special, reduced rates for nonprofit advertisers. By all means, *ask* about such rates, even if the sales representative doesn't offer them.

Radio ads "work" most effectively the more they are repeated. If it's a choice between longer but fewer ads and shorter but more frequent ads, go with the more frequent airings of the shorter ads.

In purchasing space in *newspapers* and *magazines,* know the audience you want to reach and determine what section of the publication your intended audience reads. If you are advertising your parish's classical music series, for example, "buy" the arts section of the paper. Don't limit yourself nor be limited by the so-called "church" page. Purchase your ad in the section or publication your target audience will read.

At many smaller local newspapers and radio stations, there is a relationship (although the media in question would formally deny it) between the amount of free publicity an organization receives and the amount of advertising (if any) it buys. Don't use this reality as a point of confrontation, but use it for leverage. For example, after placing an advertising order with a station, don't be afraid to ask if the station's announcers might give away free tickets to your event, or if the sales representative "thinks" there might be a good feature story in the program you are advertising.

In writing and designing an ad for the media, remember the elements of any effective message (outlined in Chapter 4). John O'Toole, in his book *The Trouble with Advertising . . .*, writes that the strategy behind writing an effective advertisement really answers three questions:

1. Who or what is the competition for our product or service?

2. Who is the person we're talking to?

3. What must we get that person to know or feel or understand in order to accomplish our objective?[13]

As a church project, your "competition" may very well be everything else in the person's life. There are so many things competing for your audience's time and attention that your ad should make clear exactly how the audience will be so much better off if they "buy" the subject of your ad.

The major mistake groups inexperienced in advertising make is that they fail to focus their ad on a single audience with a single goal. David Ogilvy, one of the acknowledged masters of advertising, says that too many advertising campaigns "are too complicated. They reflect a long list of objectives, and try to reconcile the divergent views of too many executives. By attempting to cover too many things, they achieve nothing. Many commercials and many advertisements look like the minutes of a committee."[14] Focus on a single message to a single audience. To expect your ad to do more than that is to waste your money.

It's long been recognized that good advertising personalizes a need felt by potential consumers. What need must your intended audience realize they have if they are to "buy" the subject of your ad? What can you offer your audience that no other group can offer?

Your ad's headline or opening words should include the three elements of your strategy: your intended audience, your "uniqueness" compared to the competition, and the good you offer to that audience.

## Guidelines for Approaching the Media

In playing "offense" with the media (whether electronic or print), parish communicators should observe some basic rules which can be summarized in the following "ten commandments":

1. Study your local newspapers and news media as a guideline to what local editors and news directors consider newsworthy. Then make sure that the stories you submit to them are, by *their* definition, *news*. Don't get a reputation for "puffballing."

2. *Know the audience* that a particular publication or station is trying to reach and send them ONLY news they would use—don't flood everybody with everything.

3. Remember that the media is interested in the *news* and not necessarily your parish.

4. The best approach is the *personal approach.* Get to know key media people, especially those covering your parish's ministries and interests.

5. Your best lead-in to the producer of a radio or television talk program is a succinct letter of introduction, including background information plus, if possible, a clipping or two suggesting a good news angle for the show in question.

6. Respect the media's *time* and *deadlines.* Be ready to cooperate with the media on their time schedule. Be ready to work hard and expect very little in return (it sometimes works out that way). Patience and humility are key virtues of the successful media population.

7. Use imagination and common sense in dealing with the media. Don't copycat or seek "me too!" coverage.

8. Never complain about coverage. Calmly and rationally point out only the most glaring errors that could have important repercussions for your parish or organization.

9. Remember that the media are businesses, not service organizations. They deal in the commodity of audiences. Your messages will only be considered as they relate to that medium's intended audience.

10. You cannot be effective in developing good media relations with an "ivory tower" mentality. Be an active reader, listener and viewer. Become familiar with a publication's and station's editorial content and programming for reaching their target audience. When approaching the media, make it clear to them that you understand what they are trying to do and whom they are trying to reach.

So much for the game of media relations when you are in possession of the ball. Now on to defensive strategies.

# WORKSHOP: Parish Sources for Local Media

Among news reporters and writers, sources are the gold standard.

News sources are not just the mysterious "Deep Throats" of Watergate-fame who meet reporters under the cover of darkness. Anyone who is articulate and knowledgeable in a given field can be a valuable source to a reporter.

Consider the people in your parish who work in its various ministries. You may very well have outstanding sources in such areas as counseling, the health fields, education, family relations, elderly concerns, and peace and justice issues. If the pastor has special expertise in marriage counseling, for example, or a parishioner has developed a ministry to the parish's elderly that has put him/her in touch with many of the issues important to the aged, make those individuals and their skills known to news reporters in your area. You may not be able to get your local newspaper to do a story specifically on your parish's ministry to the elderly, but your parish's expertise and experience in working with the elderly could become part of a story the paper is doing on the problems the elderly face in your region.

Among the many topics and areas of ministry most parishes can claim some expertise:

- adult education
- cultural and linguistic minorities
- bereavement and grief
- child development
- cults
- death and dying
- education
- the elderly
- ethics and morality
- liturgy and worship
- marriage and family life

- Scripture
- social justice
- widowhood
- youth ministry

Many government, corporate and educational institutions regularly distribute to the media directories and lists of the organization's personnel who are available to talk to producers and reporters about their particular areas of expertise. Consider sending your local media a list of parish "experts," with a brief outline of their qualifications and an invitation to the media to call them for information. Perhaps the Catholic parishes in your city or town or the area ministerial association could make such a guide a joint project. If your experience is like that of many other organizations who publish such listings, your booklet may inspire a reporter or editor who thumbs through your booklet to do a story on someone or some topic they find on one of its pages.

Remember, too, to send a copy to local talk shows and public affairs shows. Find out who the producers and/or hosts are, and send them a copy of your parish media guide. Keep in mind, however, that these shows are often looking for topics and guests that will hold an audience's attention and interest for a long period of time—sometimes up to an hour or two, if it's a telephone call-in show.

Remember the reporter's gold standard: Expertise, currency, responsiveness, knowledge, background and credentials are what reporters and producers are looking for in news sources.

St. Francis of Assisi Parish
12 Main Street
Anytown, U.S.A.
Telephone: 555-5555

## PARISH SOURCES
## FOR THE MEDIA REPORTERS AND PRODUCERS

| | |
|---|---|
| **Bereavement and Grief** | **Tom and Ann Kelly** (555-1234) |

Mr. and Mrs. Kelly have organized a grief counseling and grief support group at St. Francis, especially for families who, like the Kellys, have lost young family members.

| | |
|---|---|
| **The Elderly** | **Sister Joan Smith, RSM** (555-2345) |

Sister Joan has directed the parish's Senior Center for the past six years. In her work, she has dealt with the full range of issues confronting the elderly: loneliness, catastrophic illness, limited income, elderly abuse, etc.

| | |
|---|---|
| **Ethics in Business** | **Rev. Thomas Smith** (555-5555) |

Father Smith, pastor of St. Francis, holds a doctorate in ethics from Catholic University and has taught ethics at the college and seminary levels. His dissertation focused on the ethical dilemmas faced by international business.

(MORE)

**Fig. 18.**  A sample page from a parish directory for the local media.

St. Francis Parish: MEDIA GUIDE                    (page 3)

| Latin America | Sister M. Frances Breault, CSC |
| (Peru) | (555-3456) |

Sister Frances, who teaches fifth grade at St. Francis
School, was a member of the Holy Cross Sisters mission
in Peru from 1975-1981. She assisted in the parish clinic,
worked with mothers to form a sewing cooperative, and
taught religion to children.

| Linguistic Minorities; | Mary Carson |
| English as a | (555-4567) |
| Second Language | |
| (ESL) | |

Ms. Carson, an elementary school teacher, directs the
parish's ESL ministry. Over 100 Hispanic, Korean and
Vietnamese currently attend these classes.

| Marriage and | Deacon John Stuart |
| Family Life | (555-5678) |

Mr. Stuart, deacon assistant at St. Francis, is a social
worker with Catholic Charities. Marriage preparation
and working with families in crisis are the focus of both
his profession and ministry at St. Francis.

| Marriage | Len and Sheila Martin |
| Preparation | (555-6789) |

Mr. and Mrs. Martin serve as coordinators of the parish
"Toward Marriage" preparation program. Over the past
four years, they have assisted over 100 couples prepare
for marriage.

**Fig. 18.** Sample Page continued.

# Notes

1. Edgar E. Willis and Camille D'Arienzo, R.S.M., *Writing Scripts for Television, Radio, and Film* (New York: Holt, Rinehart and Winston, 1981), 98.

2. Scott M. Cutlip, Allen H. Center and Glen M. Broom, *Effective Public Relations*, 6th ed. (Englewood Cliffs, New Jersey: Prentice-Hall, 1985), 361.

3. Barth Hague, "Audience for Sale," *Media & Values*, Spring 1986 14.

4. Mary Sabolik, "Print Media: Placement Strategies for the New Segmentation," *Public Relations Journal*, November 1989, 16.

5. Cutlip, Center and Broom, *Effective Public Relations*, 365.

6. James F. Plante, "Television News: Riding the Shockwaves," *Public Relations Journal*, November 1989, 20.

7. Ronnie Clemmer, "A Short Course on Dealing with TV News Department," *The Bellringer* (Newsletter of the Publicity Club of Boston), January 1986, 5.

8. Bill Patterson, "Using Radio News Today," *Public Relations Journal*, November 1989, 22.

9. Eric Zorn, "Radio News: Alive and Struggling," *Washington Journalism Review*, December 1987, 18.

10. Richard and Deanne Mincer, *The Talk Show Book* (New York: Facts on File Publications, 1982) 44.

11. Ibid., 45.

12. Ibid., 46.

13. John O'Toole, *The Trouble with Advertising . . .* (New York: Chelsea House, 1981), 122.

14. David Ogilvy, *Ogilvy on Advertising* (New York, Crown Publishers, Inc., 1983), 20.

15. Thomas Hartman, "Booking Guest Experts for TV News," *Washington Journalism Review*, March 1984, 27.

# Chapter 6

# Media Relations II: Playing 'Defense'

Imagine your parish's worst nightmare:

*"St. John's pastor arrested for . . ."*

*"Two Sacred Heart youth group members killed on parish outing . . ."*

*"Usher admits to embezzlement of church funds . . ."*

*"Student's illness traced to parish school's water . . ."*

When a reporter calls inquiring about events and situations like these, the parish communicator is now playing media "defense." Such crises are, sadly, a way-of-life for every organization, including parishes and church organizations. These stories can cripple or destroy an organization; but, if they are handled well, they can turn out to be a blessing—a positive force both within the organization and in terms of renewing the public's faith and confidence in the organization.

The next few pages focus on defensive media strategies: how to identify a crisis and how to handle it, as well as dealing with any difficult media interview.

## A Primer in Crisis Management

In September 1982, seven people in the Chicago area died after taking Tylenol capsules laced with cyanide. To this day, nobody knows how the poisoned capsules found their way on to the store shelves.

The day before the Tylenol-related deaths, the product commanded 35 percent of the adult over-the-counter analgesic market, accounted for some $450 million in annual sales, and contributed over 15 percent of Johnson & Johnson's overall profits the previous year.[1]

The manner in which Johnson & Johnson dealt with these tragic events has become, for businesses and organizations, the model for handling such crises. Parishes and church institutions can learn a great deal from the company's experience.

The first step in averting the disaster actually took place three years before, in 1979. James E. Burke, chairman of Johnson & Johnson, initiated a company-wide effort to recommit managers to its credo (read "mission statement"), which begins: "Our first responsibility is to the doctors, nurses and patients, to mothers and others who use our products and services." Mr. Burke said that during the crisis, "nobody had to ask what the guidelines are."[2]

With that as the starting point, the company moved quickly. Mr. Burke formed a seven-member strategy group (which included the company president, members of the executive committee and the vice president for public relations) to act on rapidly developing events and to coordinate company-wide efforts. Expressing horror at the deaths, the company immediately traced the lot numbers of the poisoned packages and posted a $100,000 reward for the killer. In a series of television and newspaper ads, Johnson & Johnson offered to exchange *all* Tylenol capsules—not just in the Chicago area and not just the Tylenol in the lethal lot numbers, but every capsule, everywhere in the country, an exchange program that cost the company tens of millions of dollars. Realizing that the press was key to warning the public of the danger, the company cooperated fully with the news media.[3] Chairman Burke, himself, appeared on news programs, interview shows and on television commercials expressing the company's sorrow at what had happened and outlining exactly what the company was doing about it.

What was truly remarkable about the Johnson & Johnson media strategy was its forthrightness and compassion. There was no attempt to "stonewall" or down-play the severity of the situation. The company did not protest its innocence nor whimper about "over-reaction," though it surely might have. In the short-term, Johnson & Johnson's handling of the Tylenol scare was expensive; but in the long term, the company communicated its message that

Johnson & Johnson is a candid, contrite and compassionate company, completely committed to protecting the public, regardless of the cost. Johnson & Johnson clearly positioned itself as a champion of the consumer, gave meaning to the concept of corporate responsibility and demonstrated communication expertise that will be hard to equal for years to come.[4] Within months, Tylenol had soared back to its 35-percent share of the over-the-counter headache remedy market.[5]

In February 1986, Johnson & Johnson relived the nightmare when a 23-year-old New York woman died from a bottle of tainted Tylenol. The company handled that crisis with the same openness and forthrightness as the 1982 case. This time the company concluded—and told the public as such—that even though methods to seal the plastic capsules were improving dramatically, "there is no tamperproof package, [there] never is going to be a tamperproof package." Despite a cost of $150 million for that first year, the company decided to abandon the capsule—a product the public clearly preferred.[6] Since then the company has been marketing Tylenol caplets—and the product is doing as well as ever.

Mr. Burke, reflecting on the 1986 tragedy, said of his company's efforts: "The public knows if you're being straight with them, and they usually sense it if you aren't. That's one of the things about television. It has a tendency to reveal us as we really are."[7]

## Planning for the Worst

Poorly-managed crises typically follow a predictable pattern:

- An organization receives early indications that trouble is brewing, but . . .

- The warnings are ignored or played down, until the warning signs build to climax.

- First instinct: say nothing—the leadership is concerned over liability, nobody is certain who should speak for the organization, and often the organization is not sure what really happened.

- As the pressure mounts, leaders are so overwhelmed they can't cope effectively, so they go for the "quick fix": they stonewall, they make light of the situation, they seek to blame someone else—especially the media.[8]

In the event of a crisis, the first rule of public relations is *to tell the truth about what happened.* Lying is not only unethical, it's stupid. Once caught in a lie, you and your organization will cease to have credibility.[9]

As Johnson & Johnson team can testify, in any crisis, the *first 24 hours are critical.*[10] The strategy should be to move aggressively to explain a problem and announce immediate action to correct it.

Crises that are handled well also follow a determined pattern of action:

1. *Get all the information and facts of the situation together.* Many crises result from leadership not knowing what was going on in the first place (the Space Shuttle Challenger disaster in 1986 is a prime example).

2. *Identify the audiences and specific segments of the community most affected by or interested in the situation:* parents, the parish community at-large, the parish council, the diocesan leadership.

3. *Articulate the institution's response in a statement,* as short and as succinct as possible (ideally, one that can be read in about 30-60 seconds). Keep in the forefront how the organization's action and response to this situation is *in keeping with its overall goals and mission* (this is where a mission statement is particularly helpful).

4. *Don't lie* or "blow smoke" or stonewall. Your personal credibility and the credibility of the organization are your most valuable assets. The truth will eventually surface.

5. *Designate one spokesperson for the organization,* someone with credibility both within the organization and outside of it, someone close to the situation who knows the the issues involved. All requests for statements and interviews should be refered to this designated spokesperson.

6. When the "crisis" is over, *evaluate everyone's performance.*

The best way, of course, for a parish or organization to handle a disaster or crisis is to *plan* for it:

- Anticipate problems. Identify areas of vulnerability. Dare to conjure up worst-case scenarios—what can "blow up" and how? Consider both emergencies (fires, accidents, natural disasters) and controversial issues (scandal, protests, investigations and any situations which can adversely affect your parish's reputation). Keep a file of news stories of church-related issues currently being covered in the media, especially those issues and situations critical of the Church (financial improprieties and sexual abuse, for example).

- Once those vulnerable areas are identified, constantly monitor those areas of operation—keep an eye open for those "ticking bombs."

- Maintain good media relations. How is your credibility with the media, in the community?

- Draw up a game plan if the worst should happen:

  1. Identify a crisis-management team.

  2. Decide who will be sole spokesperson.

  3. Compile a list of key publics and telephone numbers and addresses to reach them (a good practice is to always have ready a set of stamped envelopes addressed to every member of the parish).

  4. Make sure every key person in the organization has a copy of the plan and knows what to do—and what NOT to do—when a crisis situation develops.

## Why Talk to Reporters?

At some point in the crisis situation, of course, reporters will call. There will also be times when the media will call in non-crisis but nonetheless critical situations: a reporter might call for your comment on the latest Vatican pronouncement, or to ask you to share your insights and experience on a topic on which you have been identified as a knowledgeable source.

It can happen and has happened that pastors and church officials have been burned by the media in the coverage of a news story.

## *Communications CRISIS Plan*

*RESOURCES to have at hand:*

- TELEPHONE NUMBERS of parish leaders and/or those on the parish crisis management team (*HOME and WORK numbers*)
- Set of pre-addressed stamped ENVELOPES to parishioners
- *Parish Mission Statement*

- *Step 1:* FACT-FINDING
  - Who? • What? • Where? • When? • Why? • How?
- *Step 2:* PUBLICS AFFECTED BY CRISIS

  Those MOST affected by crisis:
  > *Channels to reach them:*

  Others affected by crisis:
  > *Channels to reach them:*

- *Step 3:* RESPONSE
  - *What is being done to deal with this crisis, especially to help those most affected?*
  - Draft RESPONSE STATEMENT (*brief, 30-60 seconds*).
    Question to consider:
    *How is your response in keeping with the mission of the parish?*
  - Designate ONE SPOKESPERSON *for the parish* (*ALL media inquires should be directed to this person*).

- *Step 4:* EVALUATE CRISIS AND RESPONSE
  *What worked well, what failed, what can we do to prevent this from happening again or to be better prepared for this next time?*

**Fig. 19.** Communications Crisis

They find themselves talking with a reporter in what they thought was a friendly conversation, only to read their remarks in print later on.

Before you take that call or sit down for that interview, you should know the conventions of the news media—the "rules" that all good and responsible reporters and journalists observe in dealing with sources.

Whenever you are approached by a reporter, be sure that he or she is a reporter from a specific publication or station. Don't be afraid to ask for such identification from reporters (after all, you are identified to them) and to discuss the "ground rules" (discussed below) until you are satisfied that *both* you and the reporter understand clearly the purpose of the interview and the information to be discussed.

You should, first, understand that an individual is *under no obligation* to give an interview to the media. They are not entitled, legally or morally, to your time, nor are you accountable, legally or morally, to the media (officials of certain public institutions may be obligated to provide information, but this can be presented in the form of a prepared statement).

As Vice-President for Public Affairs for Mobil Oil, Herb Schmertz has dealt with all the major national and international media from *The New York Times* to *60 Minutes*. In his book, *Goodbye to the Low Profile: The Art of Creative Confrontation,* he advises:

> Because the reporter needs your participation to do the story, you are in a position to set up conditions that are favorable to you as the price for your participation and cooperation. Before you agree to be interviewed, consider what you'll need to protect yourself and feel comfortable.

> Most reporters will be sensitive to your needs and requirements—so long as you know what they are and take the trouble to make them clear.[11]

> Always talk to the media because you want to, or because it will be good for you or your institution. But never do so because (you think) you have to. Don't let a journalist intimidate you into talking to him by telling

you that it is in your interest to cooperate. He could be right, but the decision is yours, not his. And watch out for the reporter who argues that you might as well talk to him because he's going to do the story anyway. That's not always the case. It may be that without your help, there won't be a story. So feel free to ask the reporter whom else he's going to interview, and what his sources are, and make your own decision.[12]

But, before refusing to speak with a reporter, consider carefully the effects of a "no comment" or "unavailable for comment." True, you have broken no law in refusing to talk to the media, but how will such a response be received by the people you want to reach, the constituencies you *want* to reassure, support and build up?

## Conventions of the News Media

In general, an interviewee or source can speak to a reporter on one of three bases:

• *for direct attribution* ("on the record"): When a source speaks to a reporter for direct attribution, no conditions or limits are specified. What may be said may be quoted directly and the interviewee may be listed as a source.

*If no such conditions are set, you should automatically assume that your comments and answers are for direct attribution.*

One evening, a bishop was attending a meeting of a diocesan commission. The editor of one of the local dailies was there, not as a reporter covering the meeting but as a member of the commission. During a coffee break, the editor asked the bishop about a certain situation in one of the diocesan high schools. Thinking he was engaging in a private conversation, the bishop offered his assessment. The next day, the bishop's comments were printed in full. The moral: good news people are *never* off duty.

(An important note: Radio and television reporters using audio recorders when telephoning are required to ask permission before recording a conversation with an interviewee.)

• *background:* In complex situations, a source may provide background information in order to help the reporter fully grasp the story and prevent an inaccurate or misleading account from being reported. Both the reporter and the source must agree to this arrangement before the discussion begins (these agreements are usually made with a reporter the source knows and trusts). All statements made "on background" are directly quotable, but can not be attributed by name or title—the type of attribution must be spelled out in advance and approved by the source ("a parish spokesperson," "a White House official," "a government attorney").

• *deep background* (sometimes thought of as "off the record"): When a source speaks on "deep background," anything that is said in the interview is usable but not in direct quotation and not for attribution—the reporter takes responsibility for the information's authenticity.

The reporter can go to other sources for confirmation, but cannot identify the source in any way. Reporters generally dislike "deep background" and agree to it only in the most delicate circumstances and for urgent news (some news organizations have been "burned" by government sources who spoke on "deep background" in order to plant stories that were really "trial balloons" to gauge public reactions to actions the government was considering).

Many a source has been burned because they thought they were speaking "off the record" (like the unsuspecting bishop, above). First, understand that most reporters and editors are reluctant to enter into a prior agreement for an "off the record" discussion. Usually they will do so only with sources they know and trust. And keep in mind that what is said off the record may be used by a reporter who can use the same information if he/she can confirm it from *another* source.

Any meetings which have any semblance of a public gathering (where there is virtually no control over who may walk in or out, such as a weekend liturgy or any event in which the whole parish has been invited) are *on the record*, even though a speaker may preface his/her remarks by saying "This is off the record." The speaker's remarks are *not* off the record because the reporter present (who, remember, has encountered no obstacle to prevent his/her attending) has not consented to the agreement and because the dissemination of the information to the numbers of people who will repeat it invalidates the whole concept of secrecy.

For a meeting where there is some control over the number of participants (such as a parish finance committee) it is theoretically possible to have an "off the record" discussion. The best way to handle this situation is to announce at the outset that this meeting is an "off the record" discussion and anyone who does not share in such a consensus should leave before the business of the session begins.

If you ask in advance, most print reporters will agree to call you back and go over—for accuracy—any statements of yours they might use in the story. If the story involves delicate issues or technical information, you can take this practice a step further. Tell the reporter that you'd prefer to take down his/her questions and give the reporter your answers in writing. Because you can keep a copy of your statement, there is no need to check quotes.[13]

# Handling the Media Interview

There are a number of "tricks of the trade" that experienced sources use in responding to media requests for information and interviews:

Accept an interview for a later time or date—even if it only gets you a few extra minutes, this might be just enough time to collect your thoughts and needed facts and figures.

Keep control of the interview by sticking to the point you want to make. Reverse roles: If you were the reporter or the audience for the story, what questions or issues would you want addressed? Decide beforehand what you want to communicate and frame all your answers around that message. Build bridges from the question to the point you want to make.

Roger Ailes, who has counseled presidential candidates and executives of the nation's largest corporations on media relations, advises: "Have an agenda of three major points you want to discuss in the interview and plan to work those points in sometime during the conversation with the reporter. The most common mistake made by people who are interviewed is that they wait for the reporter to ask questions which will trigger their agenda points . . . When you're interviewed by a reporter, you shouldn't just be a backboard for his or her questions. You should gently take control, at times, to get *your* points across."[14]

In other words, sometimes you have to answer the questions that are NOT asked in order to make the point you want to make.

Mr. Ailes advises his clients "to develop three levels or 'tiers' of an answer to the most nettlesome questions you could be asked by a reporter. The first level, 'tier A,' is a one- or two-sentence summary of your position. If a reporter wants elaboration, you are ready with 'tier B,' a concrete example to back up the summary, plus a little more detail. Most reporters won't need more than two levels to an answer, but if need be, you should be ready with 'tier C,' a further elaboration using another supporting statement."[15]

Not every question is based on a correct premise. There are certain kinds of questions that are traps. Don't fall into them. Avoid, for example:

- *A or B questions:* Don't limit yourself only to the choices or options offered by the reporter.

Reporter:      "Is this a case of dishonesty or sloppy bookkeeping?"

Pastor:        "We are very pleased that our accountants caught this mistake early. That's the purpose of an internal audit."

- *the hypothetical question:* Don't fall into the trap of "What if?"

Reporter:      "What would you do if one of your staff members embezzled church funds?"

Pastor:        "At our parish we've taken steps to make sure that doesn't happen . . ."

- *absent-party confrontation:* Don't get trapped into evaluating personalities and institutions.

Reporter:      "What do you think the diocese will do about Father X?"

| | |
|---|---|
| Pastor: | "This is a very painful situation for Father X, his parish and for all of us in the Church family. I know our bishop will handle this situation with sensitivity and compassion for all concerned." |

- *repeating the "buzz" word*: Don't repeat any loaded words or phrases the questioner might use ("We are not crooks"; "We are not insensitive to the needs of people.") Reposition negative language into positive, factual terms:

| | |
|---|---|
| Reporter: | "Why does the Church insist on such a narrow, anti-woman, anti-abortion stand?" |
| Pastor: | "I hear the Church speaking up FOR the lives of those who are the innocent victims of abortion— the unborn child. I think, too, our Church speaks quite eloquently FOR women and the unborn in our support for programs like Birthright and Project Rachel." |

- *questions based on faulty premises*: Sometimes the basis for the question itself is faulty and should be exposed as such.

| | |
|---|---|
| Reporter: | "Why is this pope so 'hung up' with the evils of sex?" |
| Pastor: | "Well, that's not what I'm hearing. What I'm hearing and reading of Pope John Paul's statements is his deep concern that the basic dignity of all human beings is being denigrated by a misuse of many of God's gifts. He has spoken out on such issues as economic injustice, racism, the exploitation of our environment and, yes, sexual behavior that is destructive, manipulative and dehumanizing." |

Hostility is a no-win situation. Maintain your "cool." Be firm, correct misleading questions and information, but never do so in anger or belittle the reporter. If you can't answer a question or prefer not to, say so: "Look, I really can't answer because to do so would betray the confidence of a parishioner" or "I don't know the figures exactly, but I will get back to you" (and then, *get back to the reporter*).

And never joke—it seldom looks funny in print.

The most important factor in the interview is your attitude and your confidence. Democratic Party power broker Robert S. Strauss, a master of media relations, notes: "The press has an animal instinct that smells fear."[16]

A final suggestion: More and more interviewees, especially those who appear frequently in the media, make their own tape recordings of their interviews with the media. A tape is the best proof of truth and context. It's the best way to preserve the accuracy of the entire conversation. Simply explain to the reporter that you have a policy of tape recording every interview. Reporters who are competent and ethical will not be threatened, and reporters who are potential problems are put on notice that you will not be defenseless if they err in their reporting.[17]

## Television and Radio Interviews

As discussed in Chapter 5, time is a premium in radio and television. If you are being interviewed for a newscast (as opposed to a talk show), your interview is going to be edited. Broadcast news is an assemblage of 15-30-second taped clips called *actualities*. You may speak to a reporter for more than an hour, but only a few seconds of your interview may actually appear or be heard on the air. Planning your responses and knowing exactly the points you want to make, then, are especially important. For television and radio microphones, speak in short declarative sentences and be able to present your position in 10 seconds or less.[18] And be ready to make your point—even if it is not asked.

In appearing on television, "less is more" when it comes to your wardrobe. Dress conservatively—nothing gaudy or loud, whether it is your suit, makeup or accessories from ties to jewelry. Stick to solid shades that contrast well (blues and grays are best). Whatever patterns you wear should be muted and subtle.

When you appear on television, don't play to the equipment. Stay focused on the interviewer, even when listening. Speak to the interviewer (even address him/her by name now and then) and stay focused on the interviewer, even when listening. Always be aware that you may be on, even though you're not talking.[19]

On radio and television, your air of decisiveness (style/delivery) is as important as your substance (content/words). Be friendly, be brief, be direct, be positive.[20]

More and more church organizations are finding themselves under increased public scrutiny. Like other social institutions—both profit and nonprofit—churches are being held to an accounting for whatever actions the public considers unethical and abusive. While there have been witch hunts, there are many sad examples of mainline church organizations getting caught in scandals and improprieties, from the financial to the sexual. Jim Robinson, Managing Editor of *The Orange County* (California) *Register*, observes that the Church's usual "mystery" defense is quickly losing credibility:

> The religious establishment has too long relied on the alleged "mystery" of its faith to keep the media in the dark. While not arguing that there is or isn't a certain mystery in each person's faith, most of what the media views as religious news contains little mystery (that is, unless the church flak turns the story into an impenetrable riddle).

> Religion stories are no more or less complicated to report on than corporate proxy statements, environmental impact studies or controversies over who's telling the truth when it comes to comparing the military strength of the United States with the power of the Soviet Union.[21]

In dealing with the media, you will find that most reporters are good, honest professionals who will treat you fairly and respectfully; they will make mistakes, but they are honest ones. There are some immature, lazy and ego-driven reporters who will sensationalize any situation for the sake of a good story. Knowing who they are is the first and best tool in dealing with them.

By experience and careful preparation, just about any encounter with the media can be approached, not as a descent into hell, but as an opportunity for grace. Even in a crisis situation, when you are clearly on "defense," a carefully-planned and prepared media interview can result in a turnover, putting you in control of the ball.

## WORKSHOP:
# Related Communication Issues and Concerns

This final workshop section challenges you to reflect on four areas of parish life in which the communications principles discussed in the preceding chapters can play a valuable and creative role:

## • *Meetings*

A church leader said not too long ago that he had come to the conclusion that hell was one long committee meeting.

Consider all the meetings that take place in your parish by its many councils, groups and committees:

- Most groups fail for two reasons: there is no clear articulated purpose, or the purpose is neglected as an ongoing guide for evaluating the group's progress.[21]  Do the groups that convene in your parish know exactly why they have been formed?  Do they have a clear set of responsibilities (a "mission statement" of some kind)? Can their progress or success in meeting those responsibilities be measured?

- Do meetings have a set agenda?  How is the agenda made up, who makes it up and when is it made up?  Are meetings called that have no clear goal or agenda in mind? Do those attending the meeting know what's on that agenda *before* they arrive?

- How many people attend these meetings?  Are there too many people there (for a committee to function as a working group, often "less is more")?  Are those attending interested, contributing, committed members of the group? Are those who attend these meetings *active* participants in the discussions?  Are some people there just because they've always been there or because inviting them is the "political" thing to do?

- Is the meeting room conducive to discussion—warm and inviting, comfortable, well lighted?  Is it so big that people feel lost and impersonal in it, or is it so small that the overcrowding impedes getting any work done?

- When you facilitate a meeting, do you make positive, reinforcing statements about participants' ideas? Do you accept and encourage criticism of your own ideas?

- Are conflicts kept subject-related or do unrelated issues tend to subtract from the purpose of the meeting?

- Do you move the meeting along by framing a consensus statement after a period of discussion: for example, "What I'm hearing around the table is that we would be better off looking at new construction rather than repairs. Is my reading accurate?"

- Do meetings end with a review of what action has been decided upon and who is responsible for the tasks to be done before the next meeting? Are deadlines set and timeliness established for projects and activities to be completed?

- Are minutes kept of meetings? Are copies sent to participants within a week of that meeting?

- Do people do their "homework" for the next meeting? The business of a parish is not "busy-ness," it is action.[22] Too many sluggish, unproductive meetings can stifle and destroy parish life, instead of nurturing it.

- ## Volunteers

Many people donate the precious gift of time to the parish community. Those volunteers in leadership positions may even be taking on the total responsibility for the organization and coordination of some program or dimension of parish life.

- Are individuals approached *personally* to give of their time? Is there an effort to match people's skills and interests with the needs of the parish?

- Are new parishioners given the opportunity to volunteer, to make their skills and interests known?

- Some parishes each year hold a parish "job fair": the various ministries and service groups hold an after-Mass fair in the parish hall, with each group having a table with literature about its work and staffed with some of its members to answer questions. In those informal, no-obligation discussions, some real talent is discovered. Does your parish have any system for discovering talent and inviting volunteers?

- Do volunteers have a sense of proprietorship of the programs and events they work on? Is there some system of "accountability," of supporting and helping volunteers realize their programs' goals?

- What kind of training are volunteers given for their work? Are there opportunities for further training and continuing education for volunteers who take on leadership roles or give service over a sustained period of time?

- How are volunteers helped to understand how their gifts of time and work are part of the total mission and ministry of the parish?

- How often and in what ways does the parish recognize their service?

## • The 'Grapevine'

Every organization—especially parishes—have an unofficial *grapevine*: parish news and rumors travel along this grapevine faster than if it aired on the nightly news.

The grapevine will fill the information gaps left by an inadequate or incomplete communications program.[23] Don't try to ignore the grapevine or control it. Realizing it exists and studying how it works enables you to make it work for you.

- How well are parish leaders "plugged" into the grapevine?

- Can you identify "branches" of the grapevine according to interests and objectives? Can you identify the "leaders" of each branch of the grapevine? Do you know the "routes" the grapevine takes?

- Who are the opinion leaders in your parish? What is the basis for their influence: their professional skills? their longevity in the parish or the community? their business or political acumen?

- If the grapevine gets the news *first*, why and how does it happen? *Ideally*, how should the parish community be informed of new events and developments?

- If the grapevine gets the news *wrong*, how do you go about correcting it? Are you open to answering questions, are you calm in the face of hostility?

Studies point out that while most members consider the "grapevine" to be their primary source of organizational information, they prefer *personal* communications from their leaders and small group meetings, in that order.[25]

One parish discovered that the local supermarket was the unofficial gossip/grapevine/communications center for the parish. The parish staff soon learned how to get word to folks through that grapevine about parish activities—they also learned how to *listen* to it.

- ## Listening

  An often ignored but critical skill for communicators is listening.

  - Do you make it clear to parishioners that you welcome comments and reactions as being for *your* benefit? How do you encourage feedback from parishioners?

  - When asking for feedback, are you specific in your questions? Do you pose generalized questions such as "How am I doing?" or do you ask for specifics, such as "Is the new weekend Mass schedule working for you?"

  - Do you have regular, informal contact with the people of your parish? One pastor regularly invites two or three different couples over to the rectory for dinner and conversation—it's a good way for the pastor to get to know parishioners (especially new parishioners), for parishioners to get to know the pastor and for parishioners to get to know one another. Does your parish leadership have some kind of "listening" system or process in place?

- Every parish used to have an annual census during which the priests of the parish would meet and visit every family in their homes. Do you have any kind of visitation program in your parish?

- Do you have a reputation for candor, for leveling with staff and parishioners? Listening—that precious ability to hear the pain of those whom the parish minister is called to serve, that first gift that pastors give to those who cry out for God,—is the cornerstone of the ministry of communications.

# Notes

1. Mitchell Leon, "Tylenol Fights Back," *Public Relations Journal,* March 1983, 10.

2. Steven Prokesch, "How Johnson & Johnson Managed Tylenol Crisis," *The New York Times,* February 23, 1986, 30.

3. Leon, *Public Relations Journal,* 13.

4. Ibid., 10.

5. David Pauly with Penelope Wang, "The Tylenol Rescue: J&J rushes to limit the corporate damage," *Newsweek,* March 3, 1986, 52.

6. Ibid.

7. Ibid., 53.

8. William C. Symonds, "How Companies are Learning to Prepare for the Worst," *Business Week,* December 23, 1985, 74-75.

9. Patricia Marantz Cohen, *A Public Relations Primer: Thinking and Writing in Context* (Englewood Cliffs, New Jersey: Prentice-Hall, Inc., 1987), 135.

10. Symonds, *Business Week,* 75.

11.  Herb Schmertz with William Novak, *Good-bye to the Low Profile: The Art of Creative Confrontation* (Boston: Little, Brown and Company, 1986), 102.

12.  Ibid., 122.

13.  Ibid., 118-119.

14.  Roger Ailes with Jon Kraushar, *You Are the Message: Secrets of Master Communicators* (Homewood, Illinois: Dow-Jones-Irwin, 1988), 153-154.

15.  Ibid., 158.

16.  Charles Kaiser with Lucy Howard, "How to Handle the Press," *Newsweek*, April 19, 1982, 90.

17.  Frederick Talbott, "Taping Reporters," *Public Relations Journal*, June 1989, 22.

18.  Scott Miller, "During a Campus Crisis, Good Rapport with News Media Can Pay Dividends," *Chronicle of Higher Education*, May 14, 1986, 27.

19.  Ailes, *You Are the Message*, 160-161.

20.  Ibid., 155.

21.  James T. Robinson, "Call to Candor," *Media & Values*, Fall 1984, 8.

22.  Tim Unsworth, "Is your parish all talk and no action?," *U.S. Parish*, May 1990, 1.

23.  Loughlan Sofield, S.J. and Carroll Juliano, S.H.C.J., *Collaborative Ministry* (Notre Dame, Indiana: Ave Maria Press, 1987), 90.

24.  Scott M. Cutlip, Allen H. Center and Glen M. Broom, *Effective Public Relations*, 6th ed. (Englewood Cliffs, New Jersey: Prentice-Hall, Inc., 1985), 343.

25.  E. Zoe McCathrin, "Beyond Employee Publications: Making the Personal Connection," *Public Relations Journal*, July 1989, 15-16.

# A Final Reflection:
# Communications as Ministry

*The Word was made flesh*
*and made his dwelling among us . . .*
John 1: 14

*Have among yourselves*
*the same attitude as Christ Jesus,*
*Who, though he was in the form of God,*
*did not regard equality with God*
*something to be grasped.*
*Rather, he emptied himself,*
*taking the form of a slave,*
*coming in human likeness;*
*and found human in appearance,*
*he humbled himself . . .*
Philippians 2: 6-8

It is the great mystery and wonder of our faith that the God who made the heavens and the earth—and us—should become one of us.

The Creator humbled himself to become one of the created, to take on himself the pain, the suffering and the anguish that is so much a part of the human experience.

The story begins with God the illegitimate child, God the unwanted, God the refugee. And then, God becomes the Teacher. But he does not teach in the language of the Pharisees nor of theological concepts that defy human comprehension. In stories about wayward children, unscrupulous servants, coins, fishing nets and seeds, he reveals his kingdom. In healing society's outcasts like the blind beggar at the gate, and in the compassion he shows to the Samaritan woman, he teaches how we might heal and love one another. In his unjust and humiliating death, he shows the limitless and unconditional love he has for us, his created—us, his children.

The Incarnation—*the Word made flesh*—is the most precise and perfect act of communication humankind has ever experienced. St.

Athanasius summed up this profound mystery so succinctly: "God became like us so that we might become like him."

Throughout this text, we have been considering parish communications in terms of "audience-centered" message-sending. To be effective message-senders—messen*gers*, if you will—we must see things from the perspective of the audience; we must look beyond our own beliefs, attitudes and perceptions to understand theirs; we must enter the joys and sorrows of those unique lives into which we seek to bring God. To use Paul's terms, if we are to approach communications as a tool of ministry, we must begin with an "emptying" of ourselves.

Communications, if it is to be an experience of Incarnation, demands selflessness, courage, hard work and love. To study, to plan, to create and to send messages as discussed in these pages demands the Spirit of the One who washed the feet of his friends and the love of the One who laid down his life for his friends.

We have all seen how the techniques and strategies discussed in this book have been used to hawk, to manipulate, to pander, to hype, to deceive. The parish minister is challenged to use these techniques to proclaim the kingdom of God, to heal the broken, to announce God's favor, to reveal the continuing mystery of the Incarnation to the people God loves "...in spirit and in truth."

Into a marketplace of painful, confusing, sinful and hopeless words, God sends message-makers and messengers to make the Incarnation—*the Word made flesh and dwelling among us*—real again, and again, and again . . . .